VENETIAN REPUBLIC

Nino Zoccali

Nino Zoccali

VENETIAN REPUBLIC

Recipes from the Veneto,
Adriatic Croatia and the Greek islands

murdoch books
Sydney | London

CONTENTS

ABOUT NINO

Nino Zoccali grew up in country Western Australia surrounded by quality produce. His mother came from a family who have farmed in the region for almost 100 years. His father, a first-generation Italian migrant, grew, harvested, reared or bartered for just about everything that was ever placed on the dinner table, from artisan home-made charcuterie and tomato sugo, to the highest quality home-grown meats and vegetables. It was at this table that Nino's love for Italian cuisine began.

After completing a double major degree in Economics and Italian, Nino went on to pursue a career in the culinary arts. At 25, he opened his first restaurant, Caffe Contadino, in Margaret River to critical acclaim. In 1998, Nino moved to Sydney and not long afterwards he headed the opening team at Otto Ristorante Italiano on Woolloomooloo wharf.

Today, Nino and his wife, Krissoula, own and operate two of Australia's most loved and highly awarded Italian restaurants: The Restaurant Pendolino and La Rosa The Strand. Both restaurants reside in the stunning, heritage-listed Strand Arcade in Sydney, and boast a loyal clientele of business, political and fashion elite.

Nino is also a passionate olive oil and wine expert and his first cookbook, *Pasta Artigiana*, was published in 2012.

LA SERENISSIMA

My fascination with Venice goes back a long way. Many years ago, when I was just 21 and had completed a 12-month sabbatical in Southern Italy, I found myself on my way to London. I had a little time up my sleeve, so I asked my learned older cousin, Liliana Di Certo, for advice on what I thought would be a difficult question – where should my next stop in Italy be? I'd been to Rome and Milan several times, but hadn't ventured far beyond these cities or the southern region of Calabria, the birthplace of my father. 'Liliana, I only have a few days. Where do you think I should go: Florence or Venice?'

She didn't hesitate. 'Venice. You are going to Venice and I am going to organise it. In Florence, you have to line up to see the art. Yes, it's amazing when you get in and see it, but in Venice, *everything* is art. There's art inside and outside, everywhere you look. It's one of the most unique places in the entire world and the barrier of water has preserved her history like nowhere else. You are going to Venice.'

And so my obsession with the floating city was born. Little did I know that Venice would continue to lure and inspire me for decades to come. Since my first visit as a wide-eyed Italo–Australian boy from Bunbury, Western Australia, I've built a career as an Italian chef and restaurateur, and returned frequently. Along the way I've also fostered a keen interest in art, music and history, and nowhere in the world are these more beautifully represented and nurtured than in Venice.

Made up of 118 islands, Venice is the jewel of the Mediterranean. 'An archaeological site which still breathes life,' according to UNESCO, which rightly added Venice and her lagoons to its World Heritage Sites list in 1987. 'Venice is a unique artistic achievement ... In this unreal space, where there is no notion of the concept of "terra ferma", masterpieces of one of the most extraordinary architectural museums on Earth have been accumulated for over 1000 years.'

Putting aside population growth and a booming tourism trade, the Venice of today isn't vastly different to the Venice of the Middle Ages and Renaissance. The water that surrounds her keeps Venice separate from her neighbours, something that Venetians – a fiercely independent people – aren't perturbed by in the slightest. This spiritual and geographical independence has kept the romance of the city alive and well for generations. Venice is a floating cultural incubator. A living fossil.

But my obsession with Venice is about more than just her artistic and architectural blessings. It's about how it all came to be. How did such a small place grow to not only enjoy such unrivalled opulence, but also play a defining role in shaping the culture and cuisine of her Mediterranean neighbours? Many are unaware that Venice had a completely transformative effect on regions along the Adriatic Sea – an effect that is still very much apparent today, some 13 centuries after Venice rose to prominence.

What makes Venice's revered status so remarkable is the fact that it was born from desperation. Venice was founded in 421 AD, after refugees from Roman cities including Padua, Aquileia, Treviso, Altino and Concordia fled Barbarian conquerors for her relative safety, where they used the marshy lagoon for protection. They joined the *incolae lacunae* or 'lagoon dwellers', fishermen who made a living from the fruits of the waters.

Venice's location at the head of the Adriatic Sea, with her countless canals and waterways, ensured she was well protected from attack or invasion. But the people's proficiency on water and their unrivalled artistry in shipbuilding put Venice in a unique position, where, despite her size and population, she became an incredible facilitator of trade.

And so the Venetian Republic was born. Existing for the millennia between the 8th and 18th centuries, the Venetian Republic refers to the thalassocracy – or empire at sea – that saw Venice dominate the trade routes on the Adriatic Sea, including commerce between Europe and North Africa. The wealth generated by this dominance created the Venice we know today.

Acclaimed food writer Waverley Root, whose 1971 book *The Food of Italy* is my bible on the history of Italian cooking, scribes:

'The free state of Venice maintained its independence for a thousand years. Its power extended inland over all north-eastern Italy, and along the valley of the Po into part of what is now Lombardy; and for some 200 years it was the world's greatest maritime power. From fishermen, the Venetians had become sailors. From coastal traders, they had become navigators, sailing especially toward the ports of the Levant. From dealers with the East by sea, they became importers from the East by land ...'

And so the great water-trading empire came to largely monopolise East–West trade for generations.

LA SERENISSIMA

The importance of water in Venice's ascent cannot be underestimated. It was on water where the Venetians were most comfortable, and where their influence was most apparent. As such, the waterways throughout the Venetian Republic became the superhighways of the era, where culinary staples such as salt, pepper, spices, corn and grain were traded and via which cultural and intellectual ideas were exchanged. Water was Venice's competitive advantage, and the medium through which her artistic and fiscal wealth were born.

Venetians' lives are built around water, both literally and figuratively – from around 1000 AD the annual Marriage of the Sea ceremony saw the ruling leader, or Doge, throw a ring into the sea and vow, 'We wed thee, sea, as a sign of true and everlasting domination.' This tradition continues today.

The Venetian Republic is often romantically referred to as La Serenissima, or 'the most serene Republic'. This has nothing to do with Venice's picturesque landscape or the calming effect of the water, but rather typifies the Venetians' motivations during their reign. They didn't rape, pillage and conquer (at least not as much as other empires); they didn't want to acquire land aggressively or show the world that they were crusaders. They just wanted to make a lot of money from high-margin trading, and reinvest it back home to create an artistic icon. And this was all done, rather uniquely for the time, under the regime of a Republic, led by the Doge – an elected leader chosen by the elite classes of the society of the time.

Like water, salt was fundamental in Venice's rise to glory. Venetians produced it from their copious briny lagoons, then sold it at an inflated price around the world. This monopoly allowed the Republic to buy meat from her neighbours; corn, originally from the Americas; rice, which was harvested in the marshy wetlands near the Po River; and exotic spices from the Arab countries of the East.

As they traded and sailed down the Adriatic, Venetians learnt about new foods, crops and cooking techniques, and incorporated them into their own cuisine, while also sharing them with their neighbours. Saffron, for example, came to Venice from the East and was then diffused throughout the Veneto. Polenta – an inescapable element of Mediterranean cuisine today – also came from the East, primarily from Turkey (one name for corn in Italian is *granoturco* – Turkish grain), and was exported back down the coast all the way to the Greek islands.

But the use of fish is probably the most glaring example of the Venetian Republic's influence. Take cod, for instance...

In 1431 a Venetian ship left Crete, headed for the North Sea and Flanders, and was hit by a storm that ultimately saw the captain, Pietro Querini, and 14 of his crew taking refuge on the uninhabited rock of Sandøy, in Norway's northern Lofoten islands. For four months, the Venetians lived with Norwegian fishermen, and learnt the art of preserving cod. Querini returned to Venice with 60 dried stockfish and showed the Doges how the Norwegians dried the fish in the wind, then beat and spiced it, turning it into a soft and tasty mix. The recipe was known by the Spanish words *baccalà mantecato*, and Querini returned to Norway many times, becoming a major trader in dried and salted codfish. Today, *baccalà mantecato* is a quintessential Venetian dish. You'll see this iteration in the Veneto too, as well as *baccalà alla vicentina*, salted codfish braised with onions, anchovies and milk. Along the Croatian coast, *bakalar* is a salted cod stew with potatoes, always cooked and eaten on Christmas Eve. Head to the Greek islands and you'll find *bakaliaros* – salted cod, fried in a beer batter and used in savoury pies.

Another dish threaded throughout the territories of La Serenissima is *pastissada*. It's true that seafood dominated (and continues to dominate) the cuisines of Venice, the Veneto, the Croatian coast and throughout the Greek islands, but this meat stew has a number of interpretations throughout these territories. Venice's version, believed to have originated in Verona, uses red meat and wine – traditionally horse meat and red wine of the Valpolicella – neither of which she could produce herself. Croatia (which claims *pašticada* as its national dish) and Greece incorporate spices such as cloves, pepper, cinnamon, paprika and nutmeg – the fruits of the Republic's trade with the Ottoman Empire.

In this book I've decided to focus on the four key regions that geographically encapsulate the Venetian Republic and which each have their own distinct cuisine, albeit with undeniable Venetian influences. These are Venice and her lagoon islands; the Veneto, of which Venice is the capital; the Croatian coast; and the Greek islands formerly under Venetian rule. I've selected dishes with strong Venetian roots or influence and have taken poetic license with some of the interpretations to give them a more modern treatment, celebrating ingredients and techniques that show how, to this day, the food in this magnificent region continues to be influenced by foreign forces.

Call it fate or serendipity, but these regions managed to weave their way into both my personal and professional life long before the concept for this book came to fruition. My business partner and wife of 18 years, Krissoula Syrmis, is from Ithaca, a Greek island that became part of the Republic in the 16th century. Cristian Casarin, our restaurant group sommelier, whose first desk was a milk crate and who's worked by my side since day one, grew up in the Veneto town of Noale. One of my dearest friends, Ino Kuvacic, an amazing Croatian chef, and his wonderful wife, Mariana, continue to espouse the essential culinary link between Venetian and Croatian coastal cooking. My love for Venice and the Venetian Republic has been fed by these wonderful relationships, and I am so grateful for the culinary and cultural insights shared with me over what already feels like a lifetime.

The Veneto

BELLUNO

VICENZA   TREVISO

VERONA   VENICE

LAKE GARDA   PADUA   CHIOGGIA

PO RIVER   ROVINJ

RAB

PAG

Croatia

ZADAR

FLORENCE   SIBENIK

DALMATIAN COAST   SPLIT

HVAR ISLAND

DUBROVNIK

Adriatic Sea

ROME

NAPLES

CORFU

LEFKADA

ITHACA

CEPHALONIA

ZANTE

Ionian Sea

Mediterranean Sea

THE VENETIAN REPUBLIC

DURING THE FIFTEENTH CENTURY

OTTOMAN EMPIRE

Black Sea

CONSTANTINOPLE

Aegean Sea

ATHENS

Greece

SANTORINI

CRETE

CYPRUS

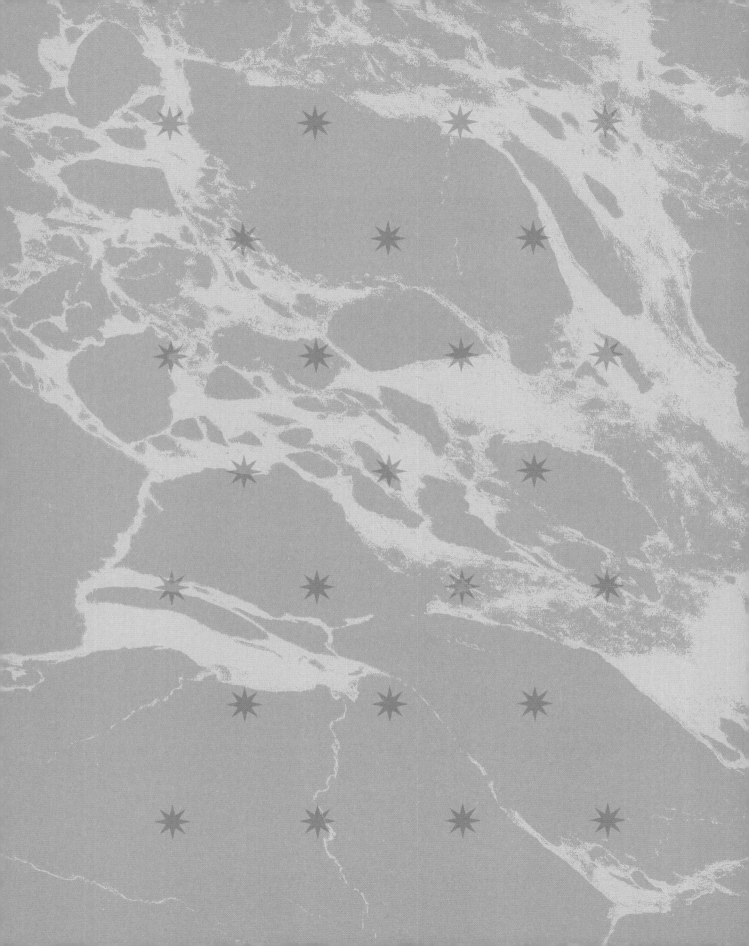

VENICE

I

FROM REFUGE TO REPUBLIC

The story of Venice is an extraordinary one, and the people who have shaped the city are unique. Entrepreneurial, tenacious, strategic and, possibly above all, proud. Throughout history they have been a people determined to see their home become unlike any other place in the world. As I mentioned in the introduction, the original Venetian 'lagoon dwellers' were joined by others seeking refuge from Barbarian invaders, and together they set about converting this marshland into the epicentre of an empire – a cultural leader beyond comparison. The Venetians wanted Venice to be a global city, and they used the wealth generated from their high-margin trading to do this, cultivating a society brimming with artistic talent and delight as they went. To my favourite author on this – Waverley Root:

'The Venetians created a brilliant society with the riches brought them by spices and commerce. Was it the effect of the exotic nature of their merchandise? "The intellectual faculties seem to have soared in an enduring exaltation under the influence of spices," Alexandre Dumas wrote in his *Grand Dictionnaire de Cuisine*. "Is it to spices that we owe [the great Venetian] Titian's masterpieces? I am tempted to believe it." Yet the Genoese dealt in spices too. They were rich too. Yet when they decided to spend their money on art, they had to seek painters elsewhere. The Venetians developed their own artists.'

By the 12th century, the Venetians were proud to be building an empire that was rapidly becoming the envy of the world, and Venice was their showpiece – a celebration of the greatest things humanity could buy, sell and, most importantly, create. Venice was becoming a centre of investment in art and culture and a place of cultivation for the finest things imaginable.

VENETIAN REPUBLIC

As one of the first international trading giants and then one of the first major tourist destinations in the world, Venice has never hesitated to take the best of what she has access to and use it to create something unique. Of course, this is more than evident in her cooking. Key trading commodities from the Ottoman Empire, including pepper, cloves, cinnamon, ginger and nutmeg, were embraced by Venice, then traded with the rest of Europe, but not before being used to help form new and exciting dishes that would go on to be considered classically Venetian.

Take *sarde in saor*, for example. While fish was historically seen as sustenance for the poor in Venice, these sweet-and-sour sardines, and similar dishes, are today a pillar of Venetian cooking. Key to the dish are pine nuts and raisins – imports from the East. *Pincia*, Venice's version of a bread pudding, is made from dried fruits, eggs, milk and usually dried bread, as well as cinnamon and nutmeg, also courtesy of the East.

If fish was the food of the lower classes, then meat – particularly game birds – was exclusively for society's upper echelons. But where did it come from? Not the East, but the Veneto to the North, where the people were far more proficient in rearing land-based proteins than their Venetian rulers, for the obvious reasons. Roast duck, veal liver with onions and both beef and equine versions of slow-cooked *pastissada* are today considered as Venetian as any dish ever will be.

Venetians are proud, but this pride has always been balanced with a willingness to admit that Venice has taken many cultural cues from her neighbours. Despite being fiercely patriotic, most Venetians will still tell you that their home has always been an international city in some way. Indeed, Venice represents everything she has touched, while she has also uniquely touched the rest of the world. Where in the Western world (and probably most of the East as well) has one not heard of Venetian glass or Venetian blinds or Vivaldi's *Four Seasons* or of two of Shakespeare's most famous masterpieces: *Othello* and *The Merchant of Venice*? Carnevale and mask-making was, and is, Venice. Where did Hemingway, Casanova and Marco Polo live? And who isn't aware of the Venice Film Festival and Biennale?

It's the same with food and wine. It's no coincidence that Venice lays claim to being the birthplace of the modern day café – Florian – the first and oldest continually trading coffee house in the world (save for the interruption of a couple of world wars). She is also home to arguably the most famous restaurant on the planet over the past century – Harry's Bar – home of carpaccio and the bellini. And let's not forget prosecco, the Veneto's international juggernaut sparkling appellation wine, made famous in Venice, and now the best-selling sparkling wine in the world.

What about produce? Whilst boutique in size, Venice's Rialto boasts one of the world's best retail food markets. Take a short boat trip to Chioggia, or 'little Venice' as it is often referred, and you'll find Italy's largest wholesale and retail fish markets.

To the deep weight of trade-driven foreign ingredients, one really needs to add another interesting impact on the cooking of Venice – that of the centuries-old influence of elite international hotel cuisine, which has become part of the culinary fabric of Venice, at times feeling more classically French than traditionally Italian. The common use of ingredients such as curry powder, mayonnaise and Cognac sets Venice apart from most places in Italy and is fortified by centuries of international hotel operations and tourism. Lobster thermidor, oysters Rockefeller, scampi americaine and beef Wellington are not uncommon throughout modern history across the lagoon isles.

Venice is all of this.

VENICE

Antipasti

FISH AND SHELLFISH CARPACCIO

Prep Time 25 minutes

2 tablespoons pistachio nuts
80 g (3 oz) swordfish fillet
80 g (3 oz) tuna fillet
80 g (3 oz) scallops
4 large scampi/langoustines
½ pomegranate
2 tablespoons lemon juice
120 ml (½ cup) Agrumato lemon
    extra virgin olive oil
2 tablespoons salmon roe
Sea salt and freshly ground
    black pepper

Named after Vittore Carpaccio, the Renaissance painter famous for his use of vivid colours, the original carpaccio dish was first plated at the iconic Harry's Bar in Venice – one of the most famous restaurants in history. At Harry's, the carpaccio has always been a raw beef dish, deeply tied to Venice and her cultural history, however carpaccio is an apt description for any raw dish *(crudo)*.

Preheat the oven to 170°C (325°F). Arrange the pistachio nuts evenly on a baking tray and cook for 6–8 minutes, or until lightly browned. Take the tray out of the oven and remove the nuts from the tray to prevent them over-colouring. Allow to cool completely before roughly chopping.

To prepare the fish and shellfish, remove any skin and blood line. Peel the scampi, then cut in half and devein: do this by using a toothpick to pierce at the back of the head to a depth of a few millimetres, then lift up the end of the toothpick to scoop out the alimentary vein. Pull the vein gently to remove.

Finely slice the swordfish, tuna and scallops and arrange on individual plates. Add two scampi halves to each plate.

Remove the seeds from the pomegranate by holding it over a bowl, seeds-side down, and tapping on the skin side of the fruit with a wooden spoon. The seeds will fall out. Remove any white pith from the seeds and scatter the seeds over the carpaccio.

Scatter the pistachios over the carpaccio. Combine the lemon juice and extra virgin olive oil in a small bowl and dress the carpaccio.

Scatter the salmon roe over the top, and season with sea salt and pepper.

—Serves 4

MIXED VENETIAN CROSTINI

This is classic *bacari* (wine bar food), served in any one of the multitude of hole-in-the-wall wine bars in Venice. A very Venetian tradition is to enjoy these bite-sized crostini during the late-afternoon aperitivo hour, when couples, friends and worn-out tourists round out the day with a selection of *cicchetti* (snacks) and *ombrette* (little glasses of regional wine). A tradition worth savouring, I say.

BACCALA MANTECATO

Prep Time 15 minutes, plus 48 hours for cod preparation
Cooking Time 35 minutes

380 g (13½ oz) *baccala* (salt cod)
1 garlic clove
1 bay leaf
200 ml (generous ¾ cup) extra virgin olive oil,
    plus extra for brushing crostini
2 tablespoons lemon juice
1 thin Italian baguette
8 black olives, roughly chopped
1 tablespoon lemon zest
1 tablespoon finely chopped parsley
Freshly ground black pepper

—Serves 4

Wash the excess salt from the salt cod and then soak it in cold water in the fridge for 48 hours, changing the water twice each day. This process will remove most of the fish's saltiness. After 48 hours, remove the fish and pat it dry with paper towels.

Place the fish, garlic and bay leaf in a large pot and cover with water. Cook over medium heat for 30 minutes. Drain and set aside, discarding the fish skin, bones and bay leaf.

Using a food processor, blend the fish to a paste, slowly adding the extra virgin olive oil in a steady stream to emulsify. Add the lemon juice and season with pepper (no salt required).

Slice the baguette into 1.5 cm (⅝ inch) slices on an angle, brush with olive oil and grill until crisp in a grill pan or cast-iron skillet on the stovetop.

Generously spread the *baccala* onto the crostini, then place the chopped olives on top and garnish with lemon zest and parsley.

TINY PRAWNS AND MAYONNAISE

Prep Time 15 minutes
Cooking Time 5 minutes

400 g (14 oz) small prawns, cooked and peeled
100 g (scant ½ cup) Mayonnaise (page 241)
1 teaspoon Worcestershire sauce
1 tablespoon lemon juice
½ teaspoon lemon zest
15 g (¼ cup) chopped chives
1 thin Italian baguette
Extra virgin olive oil, for brushing crostini
Sea salt and freshly ground black pepper

—Serves 4

Combine the prawns with the mayonnaise, Worcestershire sauce, lemon juice, zest and chives and season with salt and pepper.

Slice the baguette into 1.5 cm (⅝ inch) slices on an angle, brush with the olive oil and grill until crisp in a grill pan or cast-iron skillet on the stovetop.

Place the prawn mayonnaise mixture on top of the crostini and serve.

SARDINES IN SAOR

Prep Time 10 minutes
Cooking Time 20 minutes

60 g (scant ½ cup) pine nuts
130 ml (½ cup) extra virgin olive oil,
    plus extra for brushing crostini
8 sardine fillets
80 g (½ cup) sliced onions
70 ml (⅓ cup) white wine
60 ml (¼ cup) white wine vinegar
1 pinch cinnamon
2 bay leaves
1 sprig thyme
50 g (¼ cup) raisins
1 thin Italian baguette

—*Serves 4*

Preheat the oven to 170°C (325°F). Arrange the pine nuts evenly on a baking tray and cook for 6–8 minutes, or until lightly browned. Take the tray out of the oven and remove the nuts from the tray to prevent them over-colouring. Allow to cool completely before using.

Heat the olive oil in a large frying pan over medium heat for 1 minute, then add the sardines and cook for 1 minute on each side. Remove from the pan and place on a serving platter.

Add the onion to the frying pan and cook over low heat for 10 minutes to soften. Add the wine, vinegar, cinnamon, bay leaves, thyme and raisins and cook for 4 minutes, then pour over the sardines and allow to completely cool.

Slice the baguette into 1.5 cm (⅝ inch) slices on an angle, brush with olive oil and grill until crisp in a grill pan or cast-iron skillet on the stovetop.

Top the crostini with the sardines *in saor* and garnish with pine nuts.

SCALLOP AND CASTELLUCCIO LENTILS

Prep Time 10 minutes
Cooking Time 30 minutes

1 garlic clove, minced
1 bay leaf
1 sprig rosemary
½ onion, diced
330 ml (1⅓ cups) extra virgin olive oil,
    plus extra for brushing crostini
150 g (⅔ cup) Castelluccio lentils
½ tomato, finely diced
100 g (3½ oz) celery, finely diced
400 g (14 oz) medium-sized scallops
15 g (¼ cup) finely chopped parsley
100 ml (scant ½ cup) lemon juice
1 thin Italian baguette
Sea salt and freshly ground black pepper

—*Serves 4*

In a saucepan, sauté the garlic, bay leaf, rosemary and onion in 200 ml (generous ¾ cup) of the olive oil for 5 minutes or until the onion is translucent. Add the lentils and tomato and cover with water.

Cook the lentils over medium heat for 20–25 minutes, until tender but not mushy, topping up with water if needed. Drain the lentils, remove the tomato skins, bay leaf and rosemary and chill in the fridge.

Blanch the celery in boiling water for 10 seconds, then refresh in ice water. Drain and mix with the lentils.

Heat a sauté pan with 1½ tablespoons of the olive oil over high heat for 1 minute, then add the scallops and sear quickly for 1 minute, caramelising both sides. Add the scallops to the lentil mix, then add the parsley, lemon juice and remaining olive oil and season.

Slice the baguette into 1.5 cm (⅝ inch) slices on an angle, brush with olive oil and grill until crisp in a grill pan or cast-iron skillet on the stovetop.

Top the crostini with the lentils and scallops and serve.

VENICE ✳ *Antipasti*

MIXED VENETIAN SANDWICHES

Like the Venetian crostini, this is another classic *bacari* dish. However, in true Venetian style, these are not humble sandwiches. Bulging with a double filling in the middle and often including some of Venice's most prized ingredients, these *cicchetti* are simple but indulgent, and are best enjoyed as the sun goes down with a little glass of Garganaga or Valpolicella. Life doesn't get much better.

PRAWN, RICOTTA AND PARSLEY TRAMEZZINI

Prep Time 5 minutes

200 g (7 oz) prawn meat, cooked and cut
    into 1 cm (½ inch) cubes
200 g (scant 1 cup) ricotta cheese
2 tablespoons chopped parsley
½ tablespoon lemon zest
3 tablespoons Mayonnaise (page 241)
8 slices white bread
Sea salt and freshly ground black pepper

—Serves 4

Combine the diced prawns, ricotta, parsley, lemon zest, mayonnaise and salt and pepper in a mixing bowl.

Cut the crusts from the bread. Lay four slices of bread on the work surface and place a quarter of the filling in the centre of each.

Place another slice of bread on top of each and, using both hands, press down on all sides to seal and form a bulging centre. Cut the sandwiches in half across the centre.

TUNA, CAPER AND CASTELFRANCO RADICCHIO TRAMEZZINI

Prep Time 10 minutes
Cooking Time 15 minutes

400 g (14 oz) tuna belly
Extra virgin olive oil, to coat the fish
30 g (1 oz) anchovies, finely chopped
40 g (¼ cup) capers
80 g (½ cup) finely diced red onion
20 g (⅓ cup) finely chopped parsley
120 g (2 cups) finely shredded Castelfranco radicchio
    (or Belgian endive/witlof)
5 tablespoons Mayonnaise (page 241)
8 slices white bread
Sea salt and freshly ground black pepper

—Serves 4

Preheat the oven to 160°C (315°F).

Rub the whole piece of tuna well with olive oil, place on a baking tray and bake for 15 minutes. Allow to cool.

Break the tuna apart into small pieces with your hands and combine with the anchovies, capers, onion, parsley, radicchio and mayonnaise. Season with salt and pepper.

Cut the crusts from the bread. Lay four slices of bread on the work surface and place a quarter of the filling in the centre of each.

Place another slice of bread on top of each and, using both hands, press down on all sides to seal and form a bulging centre. Cut the sandwiches in half across the centre.

MORTADELLA, QUAIL EGG AND WILD ROCKET TRAMEZZINI

Prep Time 10 minutes
Cooking Time 4 minutes

12 quail eggs
8 slices white bread
3 tablespoons Mayonnaise (page 241)
200 g (7 oz) sliced mortadella
80 g (3 oz) wild rocket (arugula)
Sea salt and freshly ground black pepper

—*Serves 4*

Bring a small pot of water to the boil. Gently place the quail eggs in the water and cook for 4 minutes. Drain, then chill in ice water. Peel and slice the eggs.

Cut the crusts from the bread. Lay four slices of bread on the work surface and spread thinly with mayonnaise. Divide the mortadella among the sandwiches, then add the rocket and eggs. Season with salt and pepper.

Spread the other four slices of bread thinly with mayonnaise. Place these slices on top of the others to make sandwiches. Using both hands, press down on all sides to seal and form a bulging centre. Cut the sandwiches in half across the centre.

SPIDER CRAB AND MAYONNAISE TRAMEZZINI

Prep Time 4 minutes
Cooking Time 5 minutes

300 g (10½ oz) cooked spider crab meat (or any
   quality fresh cooked crab meat)
75 g (⅓ cup) Mayonnaise (page 241)
1 bunch chives, half left whole, half finely chopped
8 slices white bread
Sea salt and freshly ground black pepper

—*Serves 4*

Mix together the crab, mayonnaise, chopped chives and salt and pepper.

Cut the crusts from the bread. Lay four slices of bread on a work surface and use an eighth of the filling on each slice of bread. Place the whole chives on top of the filling, then place the remaining filling on top of the chives, making a mound of filling across the centre of each slice of bread.

Place another piece of bread on top of each and, using both hands, press down on all sides to seal and form a bulging centre. Cut the sandwiches in half across the centre.

Notes
Fresh cooked crab meat can be bought or ordered from quality fishmongers.

The bread crusts can be blitzed into breadcrumbs and used to make meatballs, coat schnitzel or fish, or sprinkle over roasted vegetables.

VENICE ✳ *Antipasti*

VENETIAN-STYLE RENAISSANCE OYSTERS
with MIXED CAVIARS, LEMON JUICE AND OLIVE OIL

Prep Time 5 minutes

Juice of ½ lemon, pips removed
150 ml (generous ½ cup)
    extra virgin olive oil
16 oysters
1 tablespoon salmon caviar
1 tablespoon trout caviar
1 tablespoon scampi caviar
    (or any caviar)
1 tablespoon sturgeon
    black caviar

This is not a dish that you'll find in Venice today, but it was prevalent in the Renaissance period, when caviar was sourced from sturgeon in the Po River and served as a luxurious garnish on oysters. At the time, Po River caviar was processed differently to how it is done nowadays, being gently cooked and then stored under oil. Lemon juice was also incorporated with the caviar in this dish, and left for a few hours before serving. Today this would be considered blasphemous as the acidity breaks down caviar – such a luxurious and expensive ingredient – which is why we suggest adding lemon juice immediately before serving. You're welcome to use as many or as few different caviars as you can source, but the colourful palette of this recipe makes it the perfect visual representation of the floating city's opulence and excess.

Mix together the lemon juice and extra virgin olive oil to make a dressing.

Top each oyster with ½ teaspoon of caviar, using different types on different oysters. Dress with a drizzle of lemon dressing just before serving.

Arrange the oysters on a large serving platter, alternating the caviars for an impressive presentation.

—Serves 4

Pasta, rice and pies

HEMINGWAY'S SCAMPI REMEDY RISOTTO

Prep Time 25 minutes
Cooking Time 2 hours

600 g (1 lb 5 oz) scampi/
langoustines, plus 2 whole
scampi to serve as a
garnish (optional)
120 ml (½ cup) extra virgin
olive oil, plus extra for
the grilled scampi
1 tablespoon chopped parsley
½ teaspoon thyme leaves
1 litre (4 cups) Fish stock
(page 236)
100 g (3½ oz) French shallots,
finely diced
320 g (1½ cups) Vialone Nano
rice (or any risotto rice)
1 tablespoon Cognac
or quality brandy
250 ml (1 cup) white wine
80 g (3 oz) butter
Sea salt and freshly ground
black pepper

Bisque
50 g (2 oz) butter
50 ml (scant ¼ cup) olive oil
1 carrot, roughly chopped
200 g (1¼ cups) roughly
chopped onion
1 celery stalk, roughly chopped
75 g (2½ oz) fennel, chopped
8 garlic cloves, roughly chopped
6 parsley stems
6 thyme sprigs
1 fresh bay leaf
8 white peppercorns
80 g (3 oz) tomato paste
(concentrated purée)
50 ml (scant ¼ cup) Cognac
or quality brandy
150 ml (generous ½ cup)
dry white wine
300 ml (1¼ cups) single
(pure) cream
1 litre (4 cups) Fish stock
(page 236)
1 pinch cayenne pepper
Freshly ground white pepper

Ernest Hemingway, like so many other cultural icons, was deeply enamoured of Venice. He was a regular at the city's famous institutions such as Harry's Bar – which actually featured in a couple of his works – and the luxurious Gritti Palace, where he always occupied the same seat. This recipe hung above that seat for many years. It's said that Hemingway self-prescribed this risotto to help alleviate pain from the injuries he sustained in two air crashes in Africa in the early 1950s.

Remove the heads and shells from the scampi and reserve to make the bisque. This will yield approximately 400 g (14 oz) of shells and 200 g (7 oz) of flesh.

To make the bisque, preheat the oven to 200°C (400°F). Mix together the butter and oil in a large mixing bowl. Crush the scampi shells and combine with the vegetables, garlic, herbs, bay leaf, peppercorns and the butter and oil mixture. Season and mix well, then place in a roasting tin and roast in the oven, stirring frequently, until the vegetables are tender and the shells are golden brown. The aroma of the scampi shells should be prominent.

Transfer to a large pan and add all the remaining ingredients except the cayenne pepper. Bring to the boil over medium heat, reduce the heat to low and simmer for between 60 and 90 minutes until the liquid is reduced by about half. Cool, then blend the ingredients in batches in a blender until smooth, and pass through a fine sieve. Season to taste with salt, white pepper and cayenne pepper.

Devein the scampi by using a toothpick to pierce the back of the head to a depth of a few millimetres, then lift up the end of the toothpick to scoop out the alimentary vein. Pull the vein gently to remove. Cut the flesh into 1 cm (½ inch) pieces and mix with 1 tablespoon of the olive oil, parsley and thyme.

Mix the fish stock and 200 ml (generous ¾ cup) of the bisque together and bring to a boil, then simmer and maintain the heat as you will be adding this to the rice.

In a medium-sized saucepan over medium heat, heat the remaining olive oil with the shallots and cook for 3–4 minutes until translucent. Add the rice and cook for 2 minutes to toast the rice. Increase the heat, add the Cognac and cook for 2 minutes. Add the wine and stir for 2 minutes or until it has evaporated.

Slowly start to add the hot fish stock and bisque one ladle at a time until the rice is al dente, stirring continually to create a creamy texture; this should take about 15–20 minutes. When the rice is just cooked, add the scampi meat and stir through, then season with salt and pepper. Add the butter and stir through.

If serving with the additional grilled scampi, simply cut the scampi in half and remove the alimentary vein. Season with salt and pepper and drizzle with extra virgin olive oil. Cook under a grill or in a grill pan for 3–4 minutes or until just cooked, then arrange on top of the risotto on a serving platter.

—*Serves 4*

VENICE ✳ Pasta, rice and pies

SPAGHETTI NERI *with* CASTRAURE ARTICHOKES AND VONGOLE

Prep Time 10 minutes, plus overnight soaking
Cooking Time 35 minutes

500 g (1 lb 2 oz) vongole or clams
200 g (7 oz) castraure baby
    artichokes (or any baby
    artichokes)
400 g (14 oz) Squid (or cuttlefish)
    ink fresh egg pasta dough, cut
    into spaghetti (page 241)
6 tablespoons extra virgin olive oil
2 garlic cloves, minced
100 ml (scant ½ cup) Sant'Erasmo
    Orto Istrian Malvasia (or any
    quality dry white wine)
15 g (½ cup) chopped
    Italian parsley
1 tablespoon butter
Sea salt and freshly ground
    black pepper

Squid (and often cuttlefish) ink is a classic ingredient in Venetian cooking, as well as in the Veneto and throughout the Dalmatian coast. It's most commonly used to braise cuttlefish or calamari, mixed into pasta doughs and stirred through risotto. In this recipe, we're partnering home-made squid ink spaghetti with two prized possessions from the Venetian island of Sant'Erasmo: baby purple artichokes and Istrian Malvasia wine, specifically Orto di Venezia, made by a revered winemaker from France, Thoulouze Michel, whose 'natural' white wine is developing quite the cult following. Of course, any aromatic white can be used instead.

Place the vongole in a container and cover with cold salted water. Refrigerate overnight to remove any sand and grit.

To cook the artichokes, simply put them whole in a pan of cold salted water and bring to the boil. Simmer for 10–20 minutes or until just cooked through to the centre (you can check this with a skewer).

Once the artichokes are cooked, remove from the water and leave to cool; after that, they are very simply prepared by gently removing the outer leaves until you reach leaves that are tender enough to eat. Trim the base of each artichoke, removing the fibrous exterior. Set aside until ready to use (they are served whole).

Meanwhile, bring a large deep pot of salted water to the boil and cook the pasta until al dente.

Drain and rinse the vongole well. In a medium-sized deep saucepan, heat the olive oil for 2 minutes, then add the garlic and cook for 1 minute. Turn up the heat to high and add the vongole and wine and cook for 1 minute to release the alcohol from the wine. Next, place a lid on the pan and cook for a further 2 minutes, shaking the pan halfway through, until the vongole open.

Add the artichokes and parsley to the pan and cook for a further 2 minutes. Add the cooked pasta to the pan and season with salt and pepper, then stir in the softened butter. Serve on a large serving dish to share.

—Serves 4

VENETIAN SPIDER CRAB PIE

Prep Time 45 minutes
Cooking Time 1 hour 20 minutes

400 g (14 oz) Fresh egg pasta
    dough, rolled into sheets no
    thicker than 1 mm (page 240)
150 ml (generous ½ cup)
    extra virgin olive oil
100 g (3½ oz) butter
155 g (1 cup) finely chopped onion
70 g (½ cup) finely diced fennel
2 garlic cloves, finely chopped
200 ml (generous ¾ cup)
    white wine
1 litre (4 cups) tomato passata
    (puréed tomatoes)
½ bunch basil leaves
1 kg (2 lb 4 oz) cooked spider crab
    meat (or any quality fresh
    cooked crab meat)
200 g (7 oz) Parmigiano Reggiano
Sea salt and freshly ground
    black pepper

Béchamel sauce
1 litre (4 cups) milk
1 bay leaf
½ onion, diced
40 g (1½ oz) butter
40 g (generous ¼ cup) plain flour
1 pinch nutmeg

Spider crab is one of Venice's most famous and abundant products. The crab flesh is absolutely stunning on its own – and Venetians enjoy it this way, usually as an entrée. It's also really beautiful in this pie, which is commonly made – and also delicious – with a variety of different fish and crustaceans, not only spider crab.

Bring a pot of salted water to the boil and cook the pasta sheets until al dente, then drain. Pat dry with tea towels and set aside.

Place the extra virgin olive oil and butter in a medium-sized saucepan with the onion, fennel and garlic and cook over low heat for 5 minutes, stirring regularly to make sure the vegetables do not take on any colour. Add the white wine and cook again for 2 minutes, then add the tomato passata and basil leaves and season with salt and pepper. Cook for 25 minutes. When cool, fold the cooked crab meat through the sauce.

Preheat the oven to 180°C (350°F).

To make the béchamel sauce, bring the milk, bay leaf and onion to a gentle simmer in a saucepan over medium heat. Strain, return the milk to the saucepan and keep warm.

In another medium saucepan, melt the butter over low heat, then add the flour and mix to form a thick paste (roux). Cook again for a further 3 minutes, stirring continuously. Slowly add the hot milk to the roux, stirring to create a smooth consistency, then season with salt and pepper and nutmeg.

To build the pie, take a 30 cm (12 inch) x 15 cm (6 inch) baking tray and spread one ladle of béchamel sauce on the base, then add a layer of pasta sheets, then a layer of the crab mix. Continue layering in this sequence, finishing with a layer of béchamel sauce. Finely grate the parmesan over the top and bake for 45 minutes.

Note
Fresh cooked crab meat can be bought or ordered from quality fishmongers.

—*Serves 6*

SALT FISH AND PRAWN RAVIOLI
with SAGE BROWN BUTTER AND PRAWN REDUCTION

Prep Time 30 minutes, plus cod preparation and chilling
Cooking Time 1 hour 30 minutes

Salt cod
500 g (1 lb 2 oz) *baccala*
    (salt cod) fillets
1 garlic clove
1 bay leaf

Ravioli filling
1 kg (2 lb 4 oz) prawns, shells on
300 g (1¼ cups) ricotta cheese
2 tablespoons chopped garlic
100 g (2¼ cups) baby spinach
100 ml (scant ½ cup)
    extra virgin olive oil
150 ml (generous ½ cup)
    white wine
Sea salt and freshly ground
    black pepper

Prawn reduction
4 tablespoons extra virgin olive oil
1 onion, chopped
140 g (1 cup) chopped celery
155 g (1 cup) chopped carrot
2 garlic cloves, crushed
1 teaspoon chopped thyme
1 tablespoon tomato paste
    (concentrated purée)
250 ml (1 cup) white wine
1 bay leaf
3 black peppercorns
250 ml (1 cup) Fish stock
    (page 236)

Pasta
400 g (14 oz) Fresh egg pasta
    dough, rolled into sheets no
    thicker than 1 mm (page 241)
Semolina, for dusting
160 g (5½ oz) butter
10 g (½ cup) sage leaves

You may or may not find this dish in Venice, but what you won't struggle to find is salt cod, or *baccala*, most traditionally in the *mantecato* (whipped) form, but also in an array of other beautiful applications, like this one, where it's paired with the delicate taste and texture of prawns. Making your own salt cod is relatively easy, and a great thing to do if you have an abundance of fish that you'd like to preserve. Bought salt cod can be lovely too – you just have to soak it in the fridge for a couple of days to alleviate the saltiness.

Wash the excess salt from the salt cod and then soak it in cold water in the fridge for 48 hours, changing the water twice each day. This process will remove most of the fish's saltiness. After 48 hours, remove and pat dry with paper towels. Finely chop the salt cod.

Place the salt cod, garlic and bay leaf in a large saucepan, cover with water and cook over medium heat for 30 minutes. Drain, discarding the fish skin, bones, bay leaf and garlic clove.

To make the ravioli filling, peel and devein the prawns, keeping the shells and heads for the prawn reduction.

Strain the ricotta in tea towels to remove all the liquid. Set aside.

Split the peeled prawns, garlic, spinach, olive oil and wine into three equal parts, keeping them separate. Place a third of the olive oil in a medium pan and bring to a medium–high heat. Place one part of the garlic into the pan, then add one part of the prawns and sauté until the garlic and prawns are golden brown. Be careful not to burn the garlic. Place one part of the baby spinach into the pan and cook until the spinach has wilted. Deglaze the pan with one part of the white wine and place the mixture on a flat tray. Repeat this process until all the prawns are cooked, then place the tray in the fridge until chilled.

Once cool, roughly process the prawns and spinach in a food processor, then add the salt cod and process until thoroughly mixed. Place in a bowl, add the ricotta and mix with a wooden spoon until fully incorporated. Season with salt and pepper.

To make the prawn reduction, heat the olive oil in a medium-sized saucepan for 2 minutes, then add the reserved prawn heads and shells and cook over medium heat for 5 minutes. Add the onion, celery, carrot, garlic and thyme and cook for a further 3 minutes.

continued...

Add the tomato paste to the pan and stir through, then add the white wine, bay leaf and peppercorns and cover with 250 ml (1 cup) water and the fish stock. Bring to a simmer and cook for 30 minutes.

Pass this prawn broth through a fine strainer into a saucepan on the stovetop and reduce the liquid to a third of its original volume. Season with salt and pepper. Set aside.

To make the ravioli, brush one sheet of the pasta dough lightly with water and place ½ tablespoon of the ravioli filling in 5 cm (2 inch) intervals. Place another sheet of pasta on top and press around the mixture to remove any air. Using a 5 cm (2 inch) cutter, cut round ravioli shapes and place on non-stick baking paper dusted with semolina.

Bring a large pot of salted water to the boil and place the ravioli in the boiling water. Cook for 2 minutes.

Add the butter and sage to a sauté pan and cook over low heat until the butter becomes a nut brown colour.

Toss the ravioli in the brown butter and then divide the ravioli among the serving dishes. Drizzle the prawn reduction over the pasta.

—*Serves 4*

VENETIAN PROSECCO AND SNAPPER RISOTTO

Prep Time 30 minutes
Cooking Time 1 hour 30 minutes

1.5 kg (3 lb 5 oz) whole red
snapper, filleted, bones
chopped and washed and
reserved for stock
3 garlic cloves, roughly chopped
6 tablespoons extra virgin olive
oil, plus extra for frying the fish
3 tablespoons lemon juice
1.1 litres (4½ cups) Fish stock
(page 236)
80 g (½ cup) finely diced
French shallots
350 g (1⅔ cups) Vialone Nano
rice (or any risotto rice)
500 ml (2 cups) La Farra Prosecco
DOCG (or any good prosecco)
80 g (3 oz) butter
Sea salt and freshly ground
black pepper

Risotto can be made with any number of white-fleshed fish, but in Venice it's commonly made with red snapper. As with all risotto, the key is the quality of the stock, which is enriched here with the snapper bones. Another classic fish risotto, *risotto di gò*, utilises whole small lagoon fish and cooks them until they almost completely disintegrate. However, most foreigners, while appreciating the intense flavours of classic dishes like *risotto di gò*, don't understand how it can be a fish risotto without any visible fish in it. As such, I've done my best to please both the traditionalists and those who eat with their eyes, including seared snapper fillets so it not only looks more satisfying, but can also be served as a substantial main course.

In a deep pot, sauté the red snapper bones and half the garlic in half the olive oil. Add the lemon juice and stock and bring to the boil. Lower the heat and gently simmer for 45 minutes, skimming regularly. Strain, return to a clean pan and keep at a simmer on the stovetop.

Cut the snapper fillets into four 150 g (5½ oz) pieces and, using a sharp knife, score the skin of the fish across the fillet in 1 cm (½ inch) intervals.

Heat the remaining olive oil in another saucepan over low heat for 1 minute. Add the shallots and remaining garlic and cook gently for 4 minutes until they are translucent. Add the rice and stir through, coating the rice with oil, then cook over high heat for a further 2 minutes. Add the prosecco to the rice and cook until the wine has evaporated.

Slowly add the hot stock to the rice, one ladle at a time, stirring continuously for around 15–20 minutes. The rice will absorb the stock and form a creamy texture.

You will need to cook the snapper before the risotto is ready. Heat a little extra virgin olive oil in a non-stick frying pan over medium heat for 2 minutes. Season the snapper on both sides and add to the pan, skin-side-down. Gently press the top of each piece of fish with a spatula for 10 seconds so the skin of the fish is flat against the base of pan – this will make the skin crisp.

Cook the fish for approximately 7 minutes on the skin side, then turn over and cook again for a further 2 minutes (depending on its thickness). Set aside to rest for 1–2 minutes.

When the risotto is ready, add the butter and then season. Cover and let the risotto rest for 2 minutes before stirring in the butter.

Divide the risotto among the serving plates and top with a snapper fillet.

—*Serves 4*

TAGLIOLINI PASTA *with* HOUSE-MADE BUTTER, WHITE ALBA TRUFFLE AND PARMIGIANO REGGIANO

Prep Time 10 minutes
Cooking Time 10 minutes

400 g (14 oz) Fresh egg pasta dough, cut into tagliolini (page 240)
200 g (7 oz) House-made butter (page 243)
4 tablespoons finely grated Parmigiano Reggiano, plus extra to serve
40 g (1½ oz) white Alba truffle, for slicing
Sea salt and freshly ground white pepper

A classic Northern Italian dish, this is also very much a staple of high-end Venetian dining. At the right times of year you'd be hard pressed to find a quality restaurant in Venice that isn't serving one version or another of this recipe. The white truffles are from Alba in Piedmont and, while not a Veneto product, they're regularly eaten across the whole of Northern Italy and are an absolute favourite in Venice and the Veneto, sitting alongside less prized black truffles from other regions. This is a dish to savour.

Fill a large deep pot with water and bring to the boil. Season with 2 tablespoons salt, add the pasta and bring back to the boil, then cook for 1–2 minutes. Drain the pasta, keeping a spoonful of the pasta water.

Gently melt the butter with the spoonful of pasta water in a large sauté pan over medium heat. Add the grated Parmigiano Reggiano and then add the cooked pasta. Stir together all the ingredients. Season with salt and pepper to taste and stir again.

Serve on a large platter. Finely slice the truffle over the pasta and finish with a final grating of cheese.

—Serves 4

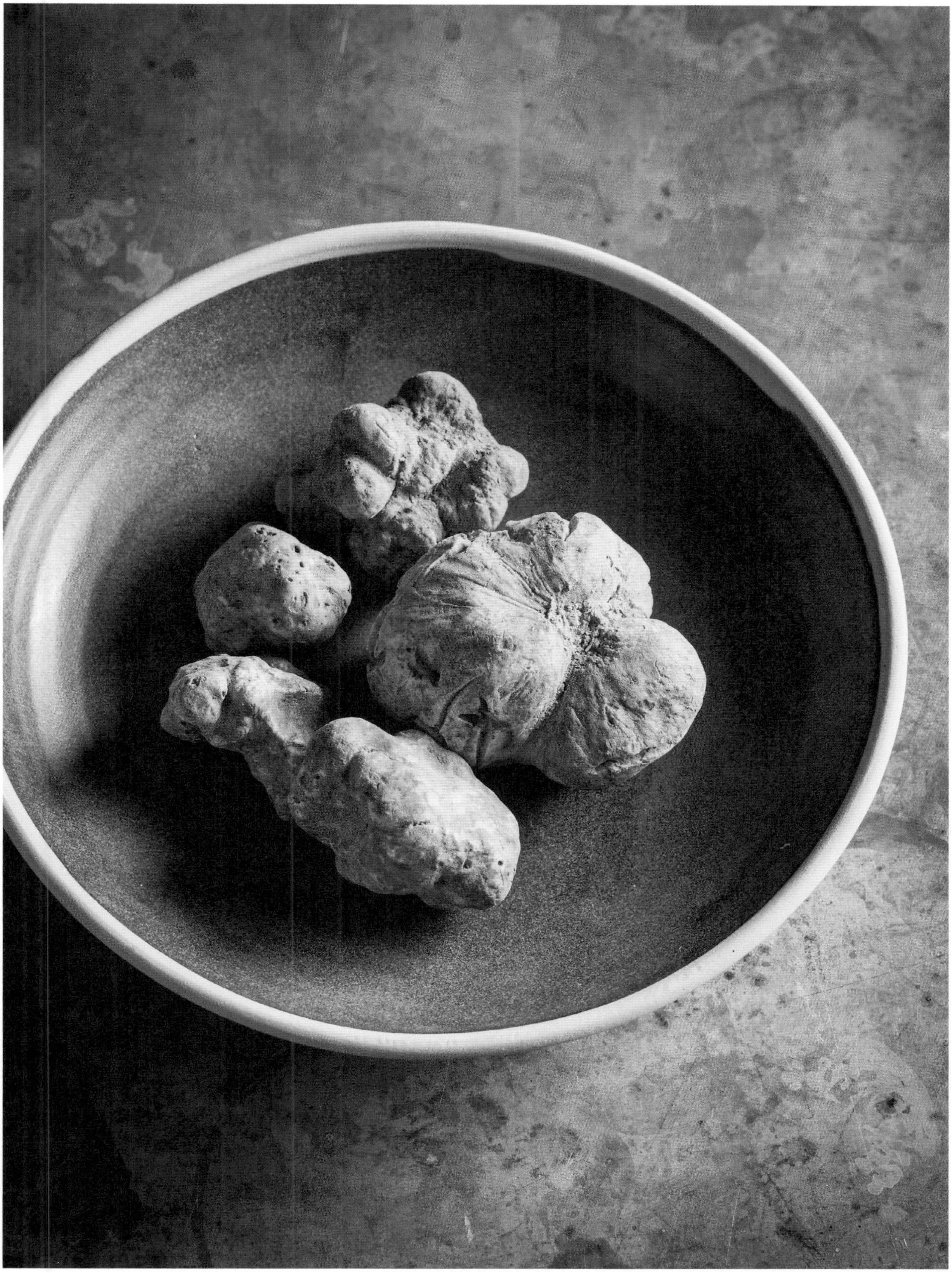

Mains

SEA PERCH 'ACQUA PAZZA' BURANO STYLE
with SANT'ERASMO PROSECCO AND CHERRY TOMATOES

Prep Time 15 minutes
Cooking Time 20 minutes

200 ml (generous ¾ cup) Lake Garda extra virgin olive oil (or any quality early-harvest extra virgin olive oil)
4 garlic cloves, thinly sliced
2 anchovies
800 g (1 lb 12 oz) whole sea perch, cleaned, scaled and gutted (or ocean perch)
250 g (9 oz) cherry tomatoes
1 tablespoon baby capers
25 g (½ cup) basil leaves
1 bay leaf
400 ml (1½ cups) Sant'Erasmo Prosecco (or any quality prosecco)
Freshly ground black pepper

Burano is a very famous Venetian fishing island that is a must-visit for any food-loving traveller. Fish served on the islands is the freshest of the fresh, coming in at all hours of the day. It doesn't get any better than at my favourite place to eat, a trattoria called Gatto Nero. Beautiful in its simplicity, this recipe hinges on the cooking of the fish, on the bone. If you get it right, the result will be beautiful and moist.

Preheat the oven to 200°C (400°F).

Place the olive oil, garlic and anchovies in a large baking tray on the stovetop over low heat and cook for 2 minutes, stirring occasionally.

Place the whole fish on the baking tray. Add the cherry tomatoes, capers, basil leaves and bay leaf to the tray.

Pour the prosecco over the fish, cover with a lid or foil and place in the oven for 10 minutes, then remove the lid or foil and cook for a further 5 minutes or until just cooked on the bone. Check the backbone at the head of the fish to see if it is cooked: the flesh should just be coming off the bone.

Season with black pepper and serve.

—Serves 2

LAGOON FISH AND SOFT SHELL CRAB FRITTO MISTO *with* WHITE ASPARAGUS

Prep Time 40 minutes
Cooking Time 10 minutes

200 g (7 oz) calamari
8 white asparagus spears
2 litres (8 cups) olive oil
1 egg, plus extra for egg wash
250 ml (1 cup) milk
300 g (5 cups) fresh breadcrumbs
30 g (½ cup) chopped parsley
300 g (2 cups) plain flour
200 g (7 oz) *moeche* (small
    soft shell crabs)
600 g (1 lb 5 oz) slip sole
    or flounder, cleaned,
    scaled and deboned
200 g (7 oz) *schie* (school prawns
    or bay shrimp), cooked, whole
    and unpeeled
2 lemons, cut into wedges
Sea salt and freshly ground
    black pepper

Horseradish cream
245 g (1 cup) sour cream
25 g (¼ cup) grated fresh
    horseradish
1 tablespoon Dijon mustard
1 tablespoon white wine vinegar

Tartar sauce
1 egg yolk
1 tablespoon white wine vinegar
1 teaspoon Dijon mustard
200 ml (generous ¾ cup)
    vegetable oil
2 tablespoons finely chopped
    French shallots
1 tablespoon chopped
    pickled cucumbers
2 tablespoons chopped capers
2 tablespoons chopped parsley
½ tablespoon lemon juice

One of the stars of this recipe is the *moeche*, or soft shell crab. An absolute delicacy in Venice – and boasting a suitable price tag – the little crustaceans are only available live for very short periods in autumn and spring. Despite occupying the Venetian lagoon all year round, they're only '*moeca*' for literally a matter of hours. During this time, the crabs moult, leaving their old shells behind in order to begin developing new and bigger ones. With very diligent fishermen watching on, the crabs are harvested at this critical time, without their shells, and rushed off to the local restaurants and produce markets – the ultimate, of course, being The Rialto Market. While *moeche* can be found snap-frozen (often the most accessible option outside Venice and the season), the classic preparation in Venice is not for the squeamish: live *moeche* are thrown into flour and fried until crispy and golden.

To make the horseradish cream, whisk together all the ingredients.

To make the tartar sauce, whisk together the egg yolk, vinegar and mustard. Slowly drizzle in the oil, whisking continually to form a thick emulsion. Mix in the rest of the ingredients. Store in the fridge until needed.

To prepare the calamari, pull the head from the calamari, cut the head below the eyes and remove the hard beak, reserving the tentacles. Using your fingers pull the quill from inside the body and peel the outer skin from the calamari. Leave whole or slice into 1 cm (½ inch) rings if the calamari is large.

Trim the asparagus, removing the woody base. You can test how far the woody section goes by bending the end of one spear and seeing where it breaks.

In a large deep pot or deep-fryer, heat the olive oil to 180°C (350°F).

Beat the egg and milk in a mixing bowl to make an egg wash. In another bowl, mix the breadcrumbs and parsley and season with salt and pepper.

Crumb the asparagus by tossing it in flour, then the egg wash and finally the breadcrumb mixture.

Cut the soft shell crabs in half, then pat dry with paper towels. Toss all the seafood separately in flour.

Starting with the larger fish (sole), place into the hot olive oil. The sole should take approximately 5 minutes. After 3 minutes you can add the smaller fish, crab and school prawns and calamari. Remove the seafood from the oil and drain on paper towels. Season with salt and pepper.

Fry the asparagus in the hot oil until golden brown. Season with salt.

Serve the fritto misto on a platter with lemon wedges, the horseradish cream and tartar sauce.

Notes
Soft shell crabs range in size from about 4 cm (1½ inches) to 12 cm (4½ inches). If the soft shell crabs are wider than 6 cm (2½ inches), they need to be cut in half. If not, leave them whole. In either case, the crabs need to be patted dry with paper towel to remove as much water as possible before being tossed through flour, prior to frying. This is really important to ensure a crispy result.

This recipe makes more horseradish cream and tartar sauce than is required. Store the remainder in airtight containers in the fridge for up to 2 weeks.

—*Serves 4*

STEAMED SHELLFISH *with* SANT'ERASMO CASTRAURE BABY ARTICHOKES AND ISOLA DELLE ROSE EXTRA VIRGIN OLIVE OIL

Prep Time 30 minutes, plus overnight soaking of vongole, if using
Cooking Time 30 minutes

12 Sant'Erasmo castraure baby
    artichokes (or any
    baby artichokes)
2 whole spider or swimmer crabs
400 g (14 oz) mussels, vongole
    or razor clams
400 g (14 oz) raw large prawns,
    unpeeled
4 scampi/langoustines
200 g (1 cup) fresh mixed picked
    wild or cultivated herbs
    (chervil, parsley, oregano,
    micro basil, micro chard)
100 ml (scant ½ cup) Isola delle
    Rose extra virgin olive oil
    (or any quality extra
    virgin olive oil)
2 lemon cheeks or wedges
Sea salt and freshly ground
    black pepper

This is another beautiful, simple dish that relies totally on the quality and freshness of its ingredients. Italians call dishes like this salads, even though they're made almost entirely of seafood and – as in this instance – include only baby artichokes as the vegetable. Feel free to use any sort of seafood or fish here, just make sure it's high quality. Do the same with the olive oil. The one I've used is a product from an absolutely stunning Venetian island called Isola delle Rose, which was built during the Fascist era and now boasts an amazing resort as well as a 100-year-old olive grove.

To cook the artichokes, simply put them whole in a pan of cold salted water and bring to the boil. Simmer for 10–20 minutes or until just cooked through to the centre (you can check this with a skewer).

Once the artichokes are cooked, remove from the water and leave to cool; after that, they are very simply prepared by gently removing the outer leaves until you reach leaves that are tender enough to eat. Trim the base of each artichoke, removing the fibrous exterior. Set aside until ready to use (they are served whole).

Prepare the crabs by removing the outer shells and then the feathery gills. Wash and chop the crabs in half.

If using vongole, soak them in cold salted water overnight to remove excess sand. Prepare the mussels by removing the beards and cleaning the shells. Prepare the razor clams by cleaning the shells.

Devein the prawns and scampi by using a toothpick to pierce the back of the head to a depth of a few millimetres, then lift up the end of the toothpick to scoop out the alimentary vein. Pull the vein gently to remove.

Next, using a large steamer or steaming oven, steam the shellfish for about 5–10 minutes or until cooked. All the mussels and clams should have opened. All the shellfish will take about the same time to cook, depending on size.

Once cooked, remove the shellfish and place the baby artichokes into the steamer to heat for about 1–2 minutes.

In a small bowl, season the herbs with sea salt and pepper, drizzle with the extra virgin olive oil and mix together.

Serve everything warm on a big platter with the lemon cheeks and scattered with herbs. The scampi and prawns can be served whole, cut in half, and completely or partially peeled. Serve with finger bowls.

—Serves 4

ROASTED VENETIAN DUCK AND PRUNES
with POTATO AND ZUCCHINI TORTA

Prep Time 25 minutes, plus 2 hours for prunes to steep
Cooking Time 1 hour 30 minutes

100 g (⅔ cup) pistachio nuts
1 deboned whole duck, skin
   on but excess fat removed
180 ml (¾ cup) red wine
3 tablespoons orange juice
4 tablespoons caster sugar
2 cloves
4 black peppercorns
1 cinnamon quill
300 g (1½ cups) pitted prunes
500 g (1 lb 2 oz) pork mince
   (30% fat)
3 garlic cloves, chopped
30 g (½ cup) chopped parsley
2 tablespoons olive oil
Sea salt and freshly ground
   black pepper

Potato and zucchini torta
600 g (1 lb 5 oz) potatoes
300 g (10½ oz)
   zucchini (courgettes)
5 tablespoons butter, melted
200 g (2 cups) grated
   Parmigiano Reggiano

Duck is one of the few stalwarts of Venetian cooking that isn't centred around fish or seafood. It is historically a regal protein, as fish was considered 'common' food for much of Venice's history. Wild duck was generally used before farmed products became available, delivering a much leaner protein. Fat (and therefore flavour) was incorporated via a process of larding – literally wrapping the duck in lardo. This recipe, albeit without the indulgent lardo, is an absolute classic, but be warned, it hinges on two things: the fat content of the pork mince (make sure it's 30 per cent) as well as the cooking time. Keep your eye on both and you'll enjoy a stunningly succulent and tender result. Wild duck can be used if you can find it, but I'd suggest larding to ensure the retention of moisture.

Preheat the oven to 170°C (325°F). Arrange the pistachio nuts evenly on a baking tray and cook for 6–8 minutes, or until lightly browned. Take the tray out of the oven and remove the nuts from the tray to prevent them from over-colouring. Allow to cool completely.

Place the deboned duck on a baking tray, season both sides and refrigerate.

In a medium-sized saucepan, bring the red wine, orange juice, sugar, cloves, peppercorns and cinnamon to the boil. Turn down the heat and simmer for 15 minutes.

Cut the prunes into quarters and place in a heatproof bowl. Pour the red wine mix over the top and let it steep for at least 2 hours.

Preheat the oven to 180°C (350°F).

Remove half the prunes from the marinade and combine with the pork mince, pistachio nuts, garlic and parsley. Season with salt and pepper. Roll the stuffing into a thick log, approximately the same length as the duck.

Remove the deboned duck from the refrigerator and place skin-side-down on a work surface, then spread open. Place the stuffing lengthways through the middle of the duck. Fold the sides over to form a cylindrical shape, tuck the ends under and, using butcher's twine, tie at even intervals along the duck.

Brush the duck with olive oil and place on a rack in a roasting tray. Roast for about 1 hour or until golden and crisp, basting every 15 minutes with its own fat.

Meanwhile, to make the potato and zucchini torta, slice the potatoes and zucchini as thinly as possible, then toss with the butter and season. In a medium-sized baking dish, layer the potato and zucchini alternately, sprinkling a little cheese between each layer. Finish with a layer of Parmigiano.

When the duck has been in the oven for 30 minutes, add the torta and bake for 40 minutes or until golden in colour.

Meanwhile, heat the remaining prunes and red wine marinade in a saucepan over low heat.

When cooked, remove the duck from the oven and cover with foil. Rest for about 10 minutes while the torta finishes cooking.

Remove the string from the duck and slice into portions. Serve with the potato and zucchini torta, the remaining prunes and the warm marinade as a sauce.

Note
Deboned duck can be found in good supermarkets, gourmet food stores or specialty butchers.

—*Serves 6*

ROASTED JOHN DORY
with PORCINI MUSHROOMS AND CRISP POTATOES

Prep Time 30 minutes
Cooking Time 20 minutes

½ lemon
800 g (1 lb 12 oz) John Dory,
    cleaned, scaled and deboned
8 g (½ cup) thyme sprigs
300 g (10½ oz) potatoes
200 ml (generous ¾ cup) Lake
    Garda extra virgin olive oil
    (or any quality early harvest
    extra virgin olive oil)
4 garlic cloves, sliced
200 g (7 oz) fresh or frozen-fresh
    porcini mushrooms (or any
    cultivated king brown
    mushrooms)
Sea salt and freshly ground
    black pepper

For me, porcini are the king of all mushrooms. I share this opinion with a lot of people, who find the flavour and texture of porcini equally amazing. Of course, porcini are particularly enjoyable fresh, but don't be reluctant to use a quality fresh-frozen product if they are unavailable – they can be difficult to source fresh, especially outside Europe. While porcini and fish is not a common pairing, the combination is fantastic when it is found.

Cut the lemon into slices and place inside the belly cavity of the John Dory with the fresh thyme. Season with salt and pepper, inside and out.

Peel, then finely slice the potatoes into 2–3 mm (⅛ inch) pieces and toss with 150 ml (generous ½ cup) extra virgin olive oil and the sliced garlic. Season with salt and pepper.

Spread the sliced potatoes and garlic evenly in a large baking tray. Place the John Dory on top of the potatoes.

Slice the porcini mushrooms in 5 mm (¼ inch) pieces and scatter over the John Dory. Drizzle with the remaining oil.

Preheat the oven to 180°C (350°F). Place the baking tray in the oven and cook for 20 minutes.

Serve the fish on a serving platter with the juices from the roasting tray, porcini mushrooms and crisp potatoes.

—Serves 2

SEARED CHICKEN LIVERS *with* MUSCATEL GRAPES, SOUR CHERRIES AND BIANCOPERLA WHITE POLENTA

Prep Time 15 minutes
Cooking Time 40 minutes

600 ml (2⅓ cups) Chicken
  stock (page 236)
95 g (½ cup) Biancoperla
  white polenta (or any
  white polenta)
4 tablespoons grated
  Parmigiano Reggiano
600 g (1 lb 5 oz) chicken livers
2 tablespoons extra virgin olive
  oil, plus extra for brushing
  the polenta
2 tablespoons butter
160 g (5½ oz) candied
  sour cherries, drained
  (or any cherries in syrup)
160 g (5½ oz) fresh
  Muscatel grapes
Sea salt and freshly ground
  black pepper

Despite the dominance of seafood across Venice and her islands, the archipelago is also very well known for its delicious handling of liver. The most iconic traditional dish is *fegato alla Venezia* – calf livers with onion – famous throughout the whole of the Veneto, if not the entire country. While not as common as their veal counterparts, chicken and duck livers are also enjoyed throughout Venice. Regardless of the type of liver you're working with, make sure you handle with care. There's nothing worse than overcooked liver – all it needs is a quick flash in the pan to create a lovely creamy and tender texture.

In a large saucepan, bring 500 ml (2 cups) of the stock to the boil, then slowly pour in the polenta in a steady stream, stirring continually. Cook for 30 minutes over low heat, then add the Parmigiano and season with salt and pepper.

Pour the cooked polenta onto a baking tray. When it is cold, cut the polenta into 6 cm (2½ inch) squares.

Using a sharp knife, remove any connective tissue from the livers, then wash under cold water and pat dry with paper towel.

Heat a large sauté pan over high heat for 1 minute. Add the olive oil to the pan and heat until it begins to smoke. Season the livers with salt and pepper, place in the pan, quickly brown on all sides then remove and set aside somewhere warm.

Turn the heat down to low, add 1 tablespoon butter to the pan and cook until nut brown. Add the cherries and grapes and turn the heat to high. Add the remaining chicken stock and cook until reduced by half. Stir in the remaining butter.

Preheat the grill, then brush the polenta with olive oil and grill for 2 minutes on each side.

Serve the polenta immediately with the livers, grapes and sour cherries.

—Serves 4

Dolci

217

CARROT, HAZELNUT AND SPELT CAKE *with* HAZELNUT GELATO

Prep Time 20 minutes, plus resting the icing, and churning and freezing the gelato
Cooking Time 45 minutes

Hazelnut gelato
670 ml (2⅔ cups) milk
145 g (⅔ cup) caster sugar
30 g (1 oz) skim milk powder
50 g (2 oz) dextrose
100 g (3½ oz) hazelnut paste

Chocolate icing
200 g (7 oz) 70% dark chocolate
200 ml (generous ¾ cup) thick
    (double) cream

Carrot, hazelnut and spelt cake
5 eggs, separated
1 pinch salt
220 g (1 cup) caster sugar
3 tablespoons hot water
410 g (2⅔ cups) grated carrot
295 g (2⅔ cups)
    ground hazelnuts
60 g (⅔ cup) spelt flour
½ teaspoon baking powder
½ teaspoon ground cinnamon
1 tablespoon rum
1 teaspoon vanilla bean paste

The land-based town of Chioggia, commonly referred to as 'Little Venice', has been very important to Venice throughout history. It supplies her with super-premium, fresh seafood (it boasts Italy's largest retail and wholesale fish market) as well as a wide array of fruit and vegetables, including its highly sought after carrots.

To make the hazelnut gelato, half fill the base pan of a double boiler with water and bring to a simmer. Place the milk in the double boiler over medium heat.

Measuring with a pastry thermometer, when the milk reaches 40°C (104°F), add the combined dry ingredients to the milk and raise the heat to 65°C (149°F). Continue cooking for 30 minutes at 65°C (149°F), stirring regularly. Blend the mixture with a stick blender, then churn in an ice cream machine to -4°C (25°F).

Meanwhile, make the chocolate icing. Place the chocolate in a heatproof bowl. Bring the cream to a simmer in a pan over low heat. Pour the cream over the chocolate and leave to stand for 30 seconds, then stir through. Cover with plastic wrap and leave at room temperature for 2 hours.

Preheat the oven to 160°C (315°F).

Whisk the egg whites and salt in a stainless steel bowl until light and fluffy soft peaks form. Slowly add 75 g (⅓ cup) of the sugar, increasing the speed to high until stiff peaks form.

In another bowl, with an electric mixer, beat the egg yolks and hot water on medium speed until light and foamy. Slowly add the remaining sugar and then beat on high speed for 3 minutes until pale and thick.

In another bowl, combine the carrot, ground hazelnuts, spelt flour, baking powder, ground cinnamon, rum and vanilla bean paste.

Fold the egg whites into the whipped egg yolks until combined, then fold into the carrot mixture in two batches.

Grease a 25 cm (10 inch) springform cake tin and pour in the batter. Bake for 50 minutes.

Remove from the cake tin and cool on a cake rack. Using a spatula, spread the chocolate icing evenly over the cake.

Note
Dextrose and hazelnut paste can be bought at quality delis and specialty stores.

—*Serves 8*

GRILLED WHITE PEACHES *with* WHITE WINE GRANITA *and* FIOR DI LATTE GELATO

Prep Time 15 minutes, plus granita and gelato freezing
Cooking Time 50 minutes

4 ripe white peaches
1 tablespoon olive oil

White wine granita
55 g (¼ cup) caster sugar
6 white peaches
125 ml (½ cup) Cavazza Durello
    sparkling white wine (or any
    quality sparkling wine)

Fior di latte gelato
650 ml (2½ cups) milk
120 ml (½ cup) single (pure) cream
145 g (⅔ cup) caster sugar
45 g (1½ oz) skim milk powder
35 g (1¼ oz) dextrose

During summer, white peaches are abundant throughout the Veneto and Venice. This recipe is all about showcasing this delightful stone fruit, so make a point of finding peaches that are at their peak of ripeness, and therefore beautifully sweet. They are fantastic with the granita, which showcases an exceptional sparkling wine called Durello, produced in the hills that border Verona and Vicenza, in an area called Monti Lessini. While any quality sparkling can be used here, the Durello boasts great structure and acidity, with lovely honey and orchard fruit aromas.

To make the granita, place the sugar and 125 ml (½ cup) water in a small saucepan over low heat and cook until the sugar dissolves and becomes a syrup.

Cut the 6 peaches into quarters, remove the stones and extract the juice using an electric vegetable or fruit juicer. You will need 750 ml (3 cups) juice. Stir the peach juice and wine into the sugar syrup.

Pour this granita mix into a tray and freeze for 2 hours. Using a fork, scrape the frozen granita to form crystals just before serving.

To make the gelato, half fill the base pan of a double boiler with water and bring to a simmer. Place the milk and cream in the double boiler over medium heat, stirring constantly, and bring to 40°C (104°F) on a pastry thermometer.

Combine all the dry ingredients, stir into the milk mixture and bring the temperature to 65°C (149°F), stirring every 5 minutes for 30 minutes.

Transfer the gelato mixture to a stainless steel bowl over ice and bring the temperature down to 40°C (104°F). Place in the freezer and stir every 10 minutes until the temperature reaches 4°C (39°F).

Place the mixture in an ice cream machine and churn to -4°C (25°F).

Preheat the grill to medium heat. Cut the 4 peaches in half and remove the stones. Lightly brush the cut side of the peaches with olive oil. Place the peaches cut-side-down on the grill and cook for 4 minutes, then turn over and grill again for 2 minutes or until softened.

Serve the grilled peaches with the granita and gelato.

Notes
Hazelnut paste can be bought from quality delis or specialty stores.

This recipe makes more granita and gelato than is required for the dish, so store the remainder in separate containers in the freezer and enjoy with fresh berries. The granita can be used as a mixer with prosecco.

—Serves 4

OSTERIA ALLE TESTIERE PISTACHIO CAKE
with PISTACHIO GELATO

Prep Time 15 minutes, plus overnight gelato cooling, churning and freezing
Cooking Time 1 hour 30 minutes

Pistachio cake
300 g (2 cups) pistachio nuts,
    skin on
6 eggs
250 g (generous 1 cup)
    caster sugar
150 g (5½ oz) butter, softened
100 g (3½ oz) potato flour starch
1 teaspoon baking powder
Icing (confectioners') sugar,
    for dusting

Pistachio gelato
500 ml (2 cups) milk
5 egg yolks
50 g (2 oz) honey
150 g (⅔ cup) caster sugar
100 g (¾ cup) pistachio nuts,
    peeled
150 ml (5 fl oz) single (pure) cream
2 tablespoons pure
    pistachio paste

Every time I'm in Venice I visit one of my favourite trattorias, Osteria alle Testiere, which serves some of the freshest, most incredible seafood I've ever had the pleasure of eating. But that's never the sole reason for my visit: Testiere's desserts are some of the very best in Venice, and none more so than their pistachio cake. It is absolute heaven and beautiful in its simplicity. It's imperative to source the highest quality ingredients, particularly the pistachios, which give the cake its lovely green colour and lightness.

To make the pistachio gelato, bring the milk to a simmer in a pan over low heat. Whisk the egg yolks, honey and sugar until thick and creamy in a heatproof bowl. Pour the milk over the egg mixture and stir until combined.

Place the heatproof bowl over a pan of simmering water and, stirring regularly, bring to 85°C (185°F) on a pastry thermometer. This should take 15–20 minutes. The mixture should coat the back of a spoon. Strain the mixture through a fine sieve into a clean container and chill overnight in the fridge.

Process the pistachios in a food processor to make a fine meal. Lightly whip the cream and fold in the pistachios and pistachio paste.

Place the chilled mixture in a gelato machine and churn until just set, then add the cream and pistachio mix and churn again for 2 minutes. Transfer the gelato into a plastic or metal container and store in the freezer until ready to use.

Preheat the oven to 160°C (315°F).

To make the pistachio cake, ground the pistachios in a food processor to make a fine meal.

Beat the eggs with the sugar. Beat in the butter. Sift the potato flour starch with the baking powder and add to the mixture gently. Finally, stir in the pistachio meal a little at a time.

Pour the mixture into a greased and lined 26 cm (10 inch) round cake tin and bake for 55–60 minutes, or until fully cooked. Test by inserting a skewer into the centre of the cake: if it comes out clean, the cake is cooked. Allow the cake to cool, then remove from the tin.

Once completely cool, dust the cake with icing sugar, slice and serve with a scoop of the gelato.

—*Serves 8*

VENETIAN CREMA ROSADA

Prep Time 10 minutes, plus flan setting and chilling
Cooking Time 1 hour

100 g (3½ oz) flaked almonds
120 g (⅔ cup) raisins
Rum, for soaking the raisins
12 eggs
150 g (⅔ cup) caster sugar
600 ml (2⅓ cups) milk
600 ml (2⅓ cups) single
    (pure) cream
4 teaspoons Rosolio liqueur
    (or any preferred liqueur
    or rum)
100 g (3½ oz) maraschino cherries

This Venetian crème caramel, or *crema rosada*, is found throughout the Veneto, in Venice and along the Dalmatian coast, and is even quite famous in Dubrovnik. Its name refers to Rosolio, the rose-scented liqueur used in the traditional recipe, but far less prevalent today. Despite the fact that nowadays people use a wide range of liqueurs or spirits – most commonly rum – the rose-inspired name has stuck.

Preheat the oven to 170°C (325°F). Arrange the almonds evenly on a baking tray and cook for 8–10 minutes, or until golden brown. Take the tray out of the oven and remove the almonds from the tray to prevent them over-colouring. Allow to cool completely before using.

Reduce the oven temperature to 150°C (300°F).

Put the raisins in a bowl with enough rum to just cover them. Set aside to soak.

In a large bowl, mix the eggs with 2 tablespoons of the caster sugar until a pale cream colour. Add the milk, cream and liqueur and combine with a spatula.

Place the remaining sugar in a small saucepan and cook over low heat for 3–5 minutes until a deep caramel colour (do not stir). Pour the caramel into a 23 cm (9 inch) diameter x 10 cm (4 inch) deep ovenproof glass bowl, covering the base evenly. Leave to set in a cool place.

Pour the cream mix into the bowl, making sure it is evenly distributed. Place the bowl in a deep roasting tin and pour hot water into the tin until it reaches three-quarters of the way up the side of the bowl.

Bake in the oven for 45 minutes: the flan should still wobble in the centre when gently shaken. Remove from the tin and refrigerate until completely chilled.

Run a small knife around the edge of the bowl, then turn out the crema rosada onto a serving plate. Serve with the rum-soaked raisins, maraschino cherries and toasted almonds.

—*Serves 10*

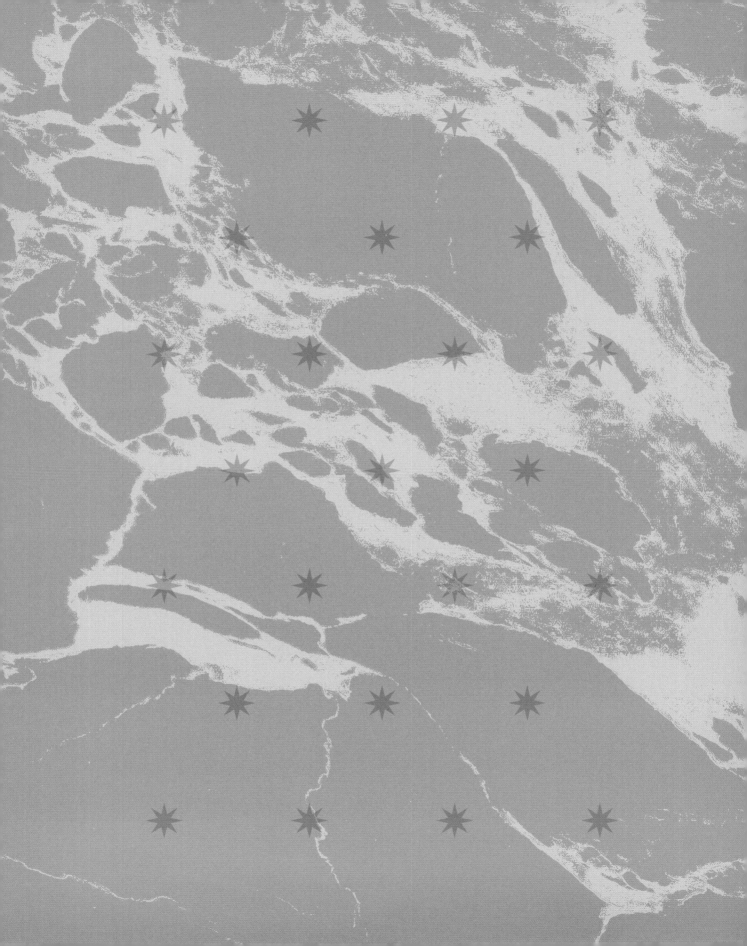

THE VENETO

II

THE LAND-BASED MARKETPLACE OF AN AQUATIC EMPIRE

With its diverse landscape and highly desirable arable land, the Veneto was the land-based jewel in the Venetian Republic's otherwise water-based crown. Today it is a treasure trove of some of Italy's finest food and wine products.

As one-third of the historical region of the Triveneto (Veneto, Friuli Venezia Giulia and Trentino Alto Adige), Veneto was a key piece of the trading puzzle for Venice. Waverley Root makes the point eloquently:

'Venice needed her hinterland not only as a market for the goods she imported from the East, but also as a supplier of staple foods like wheat, which could not be raised on her small islands; this freed her from dependence on foodstuffs brought in by sea, and made her invulnerable to blockade.'

It's clear to see how this flourishing agricultural hinterland came to form an integral cog in the wheel of the Venetian Republic. Water, however, was key again to the Republic's success on land. As has been reiterated through the ages, the Venetians were at their best on water. In order to access and take full advantage of the fruits of the Veneto, the Republic built and fortified canals and manipulated existing waterways to facilitate trade. After all, water was by far the quickest way to get around at the time – even across the land.

And, despite the Veneto region's rich resources and sheer size, she was completely dominated by Venice. What the Veneto had in agricultural prowess and natural resources, it lacked in wealth and entrepreneurialism. Venice had these in spades, and distinctively imbued her culture on the region. This is no more evident than in the cuisine of the Veneto where, unlike in any other land-based region of Italy, seafood plays a uniquely fundamental role. This is thanks solely to Venice's influence. The Po river, Lake Garda, the Venetian lagoon and the other waterways of the Veneto were, and continue to be, a rich source of fish and game meat, which have always been preferred over more land-based proteins.

Take Padua, for instance, where many of the specialties in the city, some 40 km (25 miles) from the sea, are local variants of Venetian dishes, or can be linked back directly to the Republic's trading era. Once again, seafood is prominent. *Scampi alla busara* is a popular dish, as are Venetian staples such as lagoon octopus, sardines *in saor*, fried school prawns and cuttlefish: boiled or cooked in its own ink.

Padua is even brave enough to claim herself as the real birthplace of *risi e bisi*, not a seafood dish, but one of Venice's most iconic menu items, comprising rice and (in its truest form) Veneto peas.

Moving northwest to Vicenza, which the Republic took hold of in the early 1400s, Venice's impact is impossible to avoid. Vicenza embraced Venice's culture and customs – even to the point where it was referred to as 'Venice on dry land'. Despite its inland location, Vicenza – like Venice – prefers seafood, poultry and game to the usual quadruped meats of pork, veal and beef. Its signature dish, *baccala alla vicentina*, is another treatment of the classically Venetian staple, salt cod.

Almost one-third of Veneto's surface is mountainous, and it is these regions that produce the unique artisanal cheeses, charcuterie and meats that the Veneto and Venetian people eat. The plain of the Po Valley covers more than half of the region, extending from the mountains on the Austrian border to the Adriatic, and is home to some of the Republic's most valuable commodities, namely rice and maize, from which risotto and polenta – the heart and soul of Venetian cooking – are made.

As ubiquitous as rice and polenta are in this region, so too are the various forms of the Veneto's favourite vegetable: radicchio. There are a number of different varieties, and they're treated in a plethora of different ways, both in the Veneto and her capital, Venice: grilled, roasted, braised, fried, eaten raw, tossed through salads and cooked in risottos. Where other prime agricultural areas in Italy usually offer tourists wine trails, the Veneto has an equivalent – for radicchio.

And wine is key here too, for the Veneto has historically provided the liquid fuel of Venetian society. The Veneto – where viticulture is said to have been established in the Bronze Age – is home to some of Italy's most iconic wine-producing regions, including the Valpolicella, Soave and Valdobbiadene, and contains a selection of some of Italy's most esteemed producers. We feature some of these in the following pages.

Grappa is also very important in the Veneto region where – perhaps more than anywhere else in Italy – almost every meal is sealed with a nip of grappa (breakfast coffee also often involves this ubiquitous spirit – particularly during the cold of winter).

While it's absolutely true that seafood plays a key role in the diet of Veneto people, by virtue of the region's geography it's also true that vegetable and meat-based dishes are more common here than anywhere else in the Republic. It's for this reason that this chapter focuses on the more land-based wonders of this historical agricultural territory and marketplace.

THE VENETO

Antipasti

OLIVE-OIL FRIED SCHOOL PRAWNS
with CRISPY HERBS *and* BIANCOPERLA WHITE POLENTA

Prep Time 15 minutes
Cooking Time 55 minutes

130 g (⅔ cup) Biancoperla
    white polenta (or any quality
    white polenta)
100 g (3½ oz) butter
Olive oil, for deep-frying
500 g (1 lb 2 oz) *schie*
    (school prawns or bay shrimp),
    whole and unpeeled
Plain flour, for dusting
2 handfuls picked mixed
    herbs (Italian parsley,
    sage, marjoram)
Sea salt and freshly ground
    black pepper

In and around the lagoon, *schie* (known to many as school prawns) are really, really small. They're just delightful, and this dish is an absolute crowd-pleaser. If you're not able to find *schie*, any baby or school prawns will create delicious results – just try to keep them bite-sized. Eat them whole and enjoy the crunch!

To make the polenta, bring 800 ml (3¼ cups) salted water to the boil in a large pot. Add the white polenta slowly in a constant stream, stirring continually.

Turn the heat down to low and cook for 45 minutes, stirring regularly. Add the butter to the polenta and adjust the seasoning to taste.

Heat the olive oil to 180°C (350°F) in a deep fryer or a deep pan.

Toss the prawns in the flour and shake off any excess flour. Add the prawns to the hot oil, cooking for 3 minutes until crisp, then drain on paper towel and season with salt and pepper.

Using the same pan, fry the picked herbs in batches, for about 30 seconds per batch or until crispy. Drain on paper towel.

Serve the fried prawns on the polenta, garnished with the crispy herbs.

—Serves 4

BASSANO WHITE ASPARAGUS
with MOUNTAIN HEN EGG SALAD

Prep Time 10 minutes, plus 2 days for soaking the radicchio
Cooking Time 20 minutes

1 handful mixed radicchio
and Belgian endive
16 spears Bassano del Grappa
white asparagus (or any white
or green asparagus)
4 tablespoons sea salt, plus
extra to taste
8 whole mountain hen eggs
(or any large free-range
or organic chicken or
duck eggs)
1 handful mixed field herbs
(Italian parsley, oregano, basil)
4 tablespoons Lake Garda
extra virgin olive oil (or any
quality early-harvest extra
virgin olive oil)
Shaved or grated Parmigiano
Reggiano, to serve (optional)

Valpolicella vinaigrette
1 garlic clove
100 ml (scant ½ cup) Valpolicella
red wine vinegar (or any
quality red wine vinegar)
400 ml (1½ cups) Lake Garda extra
virgin olive oil (or any quality
early-harvest extra virgin
olive oil)
Sea salt and freshly ground
black pepper

White asparagus is an absolutely stunning product of the Veneto region, and is available around the world at different times of the year. The flavour profile is different to green asparagus – it isn't as herbaceous – but this recipe is beautiful with either. It's a lovely, simple dish that lets the quality of the ingredients speak for themselves; perfect for late winter or spring.

Soak the radicchio in a bowl of cold water in the fridge for 2 days, changing the water three to four times. Drain, then set aside.

Using a sharp knife, prepare the asparagus by cutting the woody bottom off each spear. You can test how far the woody section goes by bending the end of one spear and seeing where it breaks. Alternatively, the woody ends can be peeled.

Fill a large deep pot with water, add the salt and bring to a rapid boil. Place the asparagus in the boiling water and cook for 5–8 minutes, or until just becoming tender: this will depend on the size and density of the asparagus. Remove the asparagus from the water and set aside.

Fill a saucepan with water and bring to the boil, add the eggs and cook for 6 minutes 20 seconds. Remove and peel when cool enough to handle.

To make the vinaigrette, crush the garlic with the side of a knife and rub it around the inside of a mixing bowl. Add the red wine vinegar, then slowly whisk in the extra virgin olive oil. Season to taste.

Pick the leaves from the mixed herbs, discarding the stalks. Toss the radicchio and herbs with 4 tablespoons of the Valpolicella vinaigrette and season with a pinch of sea salt. Arrange the salad on individual serving plates.

Add 4 asparagus spears to each plate. Break the eggs onto the asparagus, letting the yolks run over the salad. Drizzle with the extra virgin olive oil and season. This salad is also wonderful with shaved or grated Parmigiano Reggiano.

Note
Radicchio is renowned for being quite a bitter leaf, so we soak it in water beforehand for a sweeter flavour. In Italy a great deal of radicchio is eaten and the most bitter types are treated in a similar way before sale. Consequently, most radicchio sold in Italy is less bitter than in other places around the world.

—*Serves 4*

THE VENETO ✳ *Antipasti*

TRUFFLED VERONESE BOGONI SNAILS

Prep Time 20 minutes
Cooking Time 20 minutes

24 large European snails
2 tablespoons extra virgin olive oil
2 tablespoons finely chopped
  French shallots
2 tablespoons finely
  chopped celery
4 tablespoons finely chopped
  frozen/fresh porcini or
  fresh portobello mushrooms
2 garlic cloves, minced
1 teaspoon chopped thyme
125 ml (½ cup) Garganega white
  wine (or any quality dry
  white wine)
1 tablespoon chopped parsley
360 g (13 oz) butter, softened
20 g (¾ oz) truffle, finely grated
4 teaspoons fresh breadcrumbs
Sea salt and freshly ground
  black pepper

This dish comes from a beautiful part of the Veneto called the Euganean Hills, famous for its abundance of produce, including local truffles. The very earthy ingredients in this dish – the mushrooms and truffles particularly – are for me the taste of the Veneto, a fundamental agricultural asset during the Venetian Republic's reign. In this region, and across Italy more broadly, snails – usually synonymous with French cooking – have been enjoyed on a very regular basis and in a multitude of different ways over the years. This is just one of many, and a personal favourite.

Preheat the oven to 180°C (350°F).

Place the snails in a sink of cold water and wash, rubbing between your hands to remove any dirt from the shells. Drain and repeat the washing process.

Bring a large pan of water to the boil. Place the snails in the boiling water and cook for 3 minutes, discarding any snails that float. Drain and let cool. Remove from the shells with a small pick.

Heat a frying pan over low heat. Add the olive oil, shallots, celery, mushrooms, garlic and thyme and cook for 5 minutes, stirring regularly. Add the white wine and cook until reduced by half.

Add the snails and parsley. Season to taste. Remove from the heat and allow to cool.

Mix the softened butter with the black truffle and season with sea salt. Add the snail mix to half the truffle butter and half the breadcrumbs.

Place the mushroom and snail mix back into the shells, being sure to include one snail per shell. Seal the top of the shells with the remaining truffle butter and sprinkle with the remaining breadcrumbs.

Place the snails on an ovenproof snail platter or on a baking tray with large grain salt so that the snails stay upright. Bake for 8–10 minutes.

Notes
In many places outside Europe several ingredients for this recipe might be difficult to source. If fresh porcini mushrooms are unavailable, any fresh wild European mushrooms can be substituted.

If fresh snails are difficult to obtain, quality snap-frozen snails may be substituted and can be found in gourmet food stores.

This recipe makes more truffle butter than is required for the finished dish. You can freeze the remainder and use it tossed through fresh pasta or risotto, or to season steamed vegetables, roasted or grilled fish or meat.

—*Serves 4*

THE VENETO ✳ *Antipasti*

GRILLED SOPRESSA SALAMI *with* RED CORN POLENTA *and* TREVISO 'IN SAOR'

Prep Time 20 minutes, plus 2 days for soaking and 2 hours for marinating the radicchio
Cooking Time 1 hour

1 Treviso radicchio, quartered (or any radicchio)
80 g (½ cup) pine nuts
150 ml (generous ½ cup) extra virgin olive oil
2 white onions, sliced
3 bay leaves
85 g (½ cup) raisins
5 whole black peppercorns
5 tablespoons red wine vinegar
3 tablespoons sugar
½ tablespoon salt, for blanching
White wine vinegar, for blanching
500 ml (2 cups) Chicken stock (page 236)
95 g (½ cup) red corn (Storo) polenta (or yellow or white polenta)
4 tablespoons finely grated Parmigiano Reggiano
2 tablespoons butter
400 g (14 oz) Sopressa Veneta salami (or any fresh high fat-content salami)
Sea salt

In saor is a classic Venetian marinade, borne out of necessity rather than creativity. Traditionally used for fish – predominantly sardines – the vinegar would preserve the Venetian fishermen's meals in a time well before the luxury of refrigeration. Today, the sweet-and-sour sauce is a classic component of a number of dishes in and around Venice and the Veneto, typically combining vinegar with raisins, pine nuts and onions. While it is most commonly partnered with seafood, it can also be used with vegetables, such as the radicchio I've chosen here.

Soak the radicchio in a bowl of cold water in the fridge for 2 days, changing the water three or four times. Drain.

Preheat the oven to 170°C (325°F). Arrange the pine nuts evenly on a baking tray and cook for 6–8 minutes, or until lightly browned. Take the tray out of the oven and remove the nuts from the tray to prevent them over-colouring.

Heat the olive oil in a saucepan over medium heat, add the onion and bay leaves and cook for 5 minutes until tender. Add the raisins, black peppercorns, red wine vinegar and sugar and simmer for 5 minutes. This is your *saor* mixture.

To prepare the radicchio, blanch for 5 minutes in a mixture of boiling salted water and white wine vinegar (we use a ratio of roughly three times water to vinegar). Drain, pat dry with paper towels and put in a small bowl. Pour the *saor* mixture over the radicchio and leave to marinate for 2 hours.

Bring the chicken stock to a simmer in a pan. Season with salt and slowly pour in the polenta. Cook for 45 minutes over low heat, stirring continuously.

Add the Parmigiano and mix through. Add the butter, mix vigorously and adjust the seasoning if required.

Cut the salami into 5 mm (¼ inch) slices. Preheat a flat frying pan with a little oil and cook the salami for 1–2 minutes on each side.

To serve, place the polenta on serving plates, top with the salami and garnish with the radicchio *in saor* and toasted pine nuts.

Notes
Radicchio is renowned for being quite a bitter leaf, so for a sweeter flavour soak the radicchio in water before using, as detailed above.

The key to getting this recipe just right is sourcing a high-fat salami that's fresh and moist. We've used Sopressa Veneta salami, but any high-quality, high-fat salami can be substituted.

—Serves 4

THE VENETO ✳ *Antipasti*

Pasta, rice and pies

BASSANO RADICCHIO, VESPAIOLO AND STRACCHINO RISOTTO

Prep Time 15 minutes, plus 2 days for soaking the radicchio
Cooking Time 30 minutes

60 g (1 cup) radicchio, chopped
  into 1 cm (½ inch) squares
50 ml (scant ¼ cup) olive oil
3 French shallots, finely diced
1 garlic clove, finely sliced
350 g (1⅔ cups) Vialone
  Nano rice (or any risotto rice)
200 ml (generous ¾ cup)
  Vespaiolo white wine
  (or any good dry white wine)
800 ml (3¼ cups) Chicken or
  Vegetable stock (page 236–7)
200 g (7 oz) Stracchino cheese
  (Morlacco cheese should
  be used if available)
Sea salt and freshly ground
  black pepper
Grated Parmigiano Reggiano,
  to serve (optional)

This recipe is traditionally made with a very typical local wine, Vespaiolo, as well as another gorgeous local product, Morlacco – Stracchino cheese that has been aged for between 20 days and 3 months. This dish is beautiful with Stracchino, but is taken to another level with the aged cheese. Morlacco is rarely found outside Italy, but give it your best shot at your gourmet deli or specialty food store.

Soak the radicchio in a bowl of cold water in the fridge for 2 days, changing the water three or four times. Drain, then blanch the radicchio for 5 minutes in a pan of lightly salted water. Drain and set aside.

Heat the olive oil in a heavy-based pan over low heat for 1 minute. Add the French shallots and garlic and cook for 3 minutes, stirring continuously.

Add the rice and cook, stirring, until the rice is translucent and fully coated with oil. Stir in the white wine and cook for 2 minutes.

In a separate saucepan, bring the stock to the boil, then reduce to a simmer.

Slowly add the hot stock to the rice, one ladle at a time, stirring continuously for around 15–20 minutes. The rice will absorb the stock and form a creamy texture.

Spoon the Stracchino cheese and radicchio into the rice and mix through. Adjust the seasoning, if required.

Turn off the heat, cover the pan with a lid and leave for 3 minutes before serving. For those who really like cheese, freshly grated Parmigiano Reggiano can be added to the plates.

Note
Radicchio is renowned for being quite a bitter leaf, so for a sweeter flavour soak the radicchio in water before using, as detailed above.

—Serves 4

MARIO AND ROSALIA'S WILD HOP AND FIELD HERB RISOTTO

Prep Time 10 minutes
Cooking Time 30 minutes

200 g (7 oz) wild hops (or wild or cultivated asparagus)
75 ml (⅓ cup) extra virgin olive oil
1 large onion, finely diced
1 litre (4 cups) Chicken or Vegetable stock (page 236–7)
1 French shallot, finely diced
320 g (1½ cups) Vialone Nano rice (or any risotto rice)
20 g (1 cup) Carletti leaves (or baby spinach)
100 g (1 cup) grated Parmigiano Reggiano
60 g (2 oz) butter, softened
Sea salt and freshly ground black pepper

Every year our group sommelier, Cristian Casarin, and I travel to Italy to sample new wines and develop the restaurants' wine lists, and we always make an effort to stop off at his parents' house in the Veneto town of Noale. This dish has been eaten at their kitchen table on many occasions. When we're there – around Easter time – wild hops (which look like wheat) are plentiful, growing on the sides of the road and all throughout Mario and Rosalia's property. We'll meander around, picking what's needed for lunch, then catch up on the events of the year gone by. It's a joy. The core ingredients can be difficult to obtain outside Italy, but are wonderful if you can get them. Alternatively, wild or cultivated asparagus and baby spinach make great substitutes.

Chop the wild hops into 3 cm (1¼ inch) long pieces (smaller if using wild or cultivated asparagus). Heat half the olive oil in a small sauté pan over medium heat. Add the onion and wild hops and cook until the onion is golden, then remove from the pan.

Bring the stock to the boil in a large saucepan, then reduce the heat and keep at a simmer.

Heat the rest of the olive oil and the shallot in a large saucepan and cook for a few minutes until the shallot becomes translucent. Add the rice and toast over low heat for 2 minutes.

Slowly add the hot stock to the rice one ladle at a time, stirring continuously. After around 8 minutes, add the sautéed hops and onion, then continue stirring and adding the stock for a further 8–10 minutes, until the rice is al dente or at your preferred level of tenderness.

Turn off the heat, add the Carletti leaves and half the Parmigiano Reggiano and season, if required. Stir well, then add the butter. Cover and leave for 3 minutes. Stir the butter through the risotto and serve with the remaining cheese.

—*Serves 4*

BIGOLI PASTA *with* LAKE GARDA DUCK SAUCE

Prep Time 20 minutes
Cooking Time 1 hour 45 minutes

125 ml (½ cup) extra virgin olive oil
150 g (5½ oz) butter, diced
1 kg (2 lb 4 oz) duck marylands
155 g (1 cup) finely diced onion
80 g (½ cup) finely diced carrot
70 g (½ cup) finely diced celery
2 garlic cloves, finely diced
250 ml (1 cup) Custoza white wine (or any fruity dry white wine)
800 ml (3¼ cups) Chicken stock (page 236)
2 sprigs rosemary
2 sage leaves
2 bay leaves
4 tablespoons milk
400 g (14 oz) wholemeal Bigoli dried pasta (or any large-sized wholemeal spaghetti)
Sea salt and freshly ground black pepper
Freshly grated Parmigiano Reggiano, to serve

One of my favourite places in Italy is Lake Garda in the Veneto – particularly a little town called Costermano. The region is famous for its production of high-quality extra virgin olive oil – a long-term passion of mine. And while the towns in this area have a predominantly fish-based cuisine, much like the Venetians, they're also very big on game meat, especially duck.

Place the olive oil and half the butter in a large casserole dish over medium heat for 2 minutes. Add the duck marylands and brown evenly on all sides.

Remove the duck and add the onion, carrot, celery and garlic. Cook until the onion and vegetables become translucent. Season with salt and pepper.

Add the white wine and cook for a further 2 minutes, then add the chicken stock, rosemary, sage leaves, bay leaves and milk. Return the duck to the casserole dish. Continue cooking over low heat for 50–70 minutes or until the duck is tender. Lift out the duck and shred the meat, discarding the bones.

Cook the liquid in the casserole dish for a further 15–25 minutes until it thickens to a sauce consistency. Add the shredded duck meat to the sauce.

Bring a large pan of salted water to a rapid boil and cook the pasta for 6 minutes (to al dente) or longer, to your taste. Drain the pasta, toss with the duck ragu and stir in the remaining diced butter.

Serve with the freshly grated Parmigiano Reggiano.

Note
For an even more traditional version of this, use lard instead of butter to sauté the duck and vegetables. You can also add a small amount of cooked and chopped duck liver and giblets to the casserole with the duck meat.

—Serves 4

PUMPKIN AND RICOTTA GNOCCHI *with* BLACK TRUFFLE, BURNT BUTTER AND PARMIGIANO REGGIANO

Prep Time 25 minutes
Cooking Time 45 minutes

350 g (12 oz) pumpkin
250 g (generous 1 cup) ricotta
2 eggs
25 g (¼ cup) finely grated
    pecorino cheese
2 teaspoons sea salt
110 g (¾ cup) 00 flour
4 tablespoons butter
10 g (½ cup) sage leaves
4 tablespoons Parmigiano
    Reggiano cheese
1 piece truffle (at least 20 g/¾ oz)

This dish is an absolute joy, but it's also a labour of love. Key to getting it right is ensuring you remove as much liquid as you can from the ricotta and the pumpkin, by pat-drying with tea towels. As with any Northern Italian gnocchi, you want to avoid adding too much flour, so the more moisture you can remove, the softer and more pillowy your gnocchi will be. Have a few tea towels on hand and set some time aside. Trust me, it'll be worth the effort, and the laundry. In Italy, Berici Hills black truffles are used in this dish, but any quality black truffle will be delicious.

Preheat the oven to 180°C (350°F).

Cut the pumpkin in half, remove the seeds, place on a baking tray and bake for 35–40 minutes or until completely soft.

Using a spoon, scrape out the flesh to give you 250 g (9 oz) pumpkin pulp. Pat dry with tea towels as much as possible. Drain the ricotta cheese and, like the pumpkin, pat dry with tea towels as much as possible.

Place the pumpkin, ricotta, eggs, pecorino and sea salt in a large bowl and mix together with your hands until you have a very sticky dough. Add the flour and gently fold through to make a pliable dough. If the mix is too wet, the dough will require more flour: this can make the gnocchi harder though, so add cautiously.

Separate the dough into four equal parts and roll into logs. Using a knife, cut each one into 2.5 cm (1 inch) pieces. With the back of a fork or a wooden gnocchi tool, press each piece gently into the fork or tool to make an indentation.

Bring a large pan of water to the boil and add the gnocchi. When the gnocchi is cooked it will rise to the surface – lift out with a strainer spoon as it floats up and drain carefully.

Meanwhile, heat the butter and sage leaves in a frying pan over medium heat. Cook until the butter is nutty brown and the sage is crisp.

Arrange the gnocchi on serving plates, sprinkle with the Parmigiano Reggiano and spoon the brown butter and sage over the top. Shave black truffle over each plate and serve.

—Serves 4

RECIOTO RED WINE RISOTTO *with* LARDO

Prep Time 10 minutes
Cooking Time 35 minutes

750 ml (3 cups) Valpolicella Recioto red dessert wine (or any similar semi-sweet red dessert wine)
100 ml (scant ½ cup) olive oil
4 French shallots, chopped
2 garlic cloves, finely sliced
350 g (1⅔ cups) Vialone Nano rice (or any risotto rice)
800 ml (3¼ cups) Chicken stock (page 236)
100 g (3½ oz) Grana Padano cheese
80 g (3 oz) butter, diced
120 g (4 oz) lardo, thinly sliced into 16 slices
Sea salt and freshly ground black pepper

This is my interpretation of the classic Veneto dish, *risotto all'Amarone*. Humbly, I prefer this one. Firstly, it requires less wine because the sweetness of the Recioto carries through the dish, and secondly, the lardo adds a beautiful saltiness and an element of indulgence. While lardo is definitely used in the Valpolicella region – where the dish originates – you'd be hard pressed to find it utilised in this way. But, blasphemous as it may be, classics can be improved! I've cooked this dish for several Venetians, and they love it.

Pour 500 ml (2 cups) of the Recioto into a small saucepan and bring to a simmer over low heat. Gently simmer until the wine has reduced by half. Allow to cool.

Heat the olive oil in a heavy-based pan over low heat for 1 minute. Add the shallots and garlic and cook, stirring, for 3 minutes. Stir in the rice and continue cooking until the rice is translucent and fully coated in oil. Stir in the remaining cupful of Recioto and cook for 2 minutes.

Meanwhile, bring the chicken stock to the boil in another pan, then reduce to a simmer.

Slowly add the hot chicken stock to the rice, one ladle at a time, stirring continuously for 15–20 minutes until the rice has absorbed the stock and has a creamy texture.

Grate the Grana Padano into the risotto and mix through. Add the butter, stir vigorously, then season with salt and pepper. Turn the heat off, cover the pan with a lid and leave for 3 minutes.

Spoon the risotto onto serving plates. Lay four slices of lardo over the top of each portion, then finish with a drizzle of the Recioto reduction.

—Serves 4

GAME AND MOUNTAIN HERB TORTELLINI
with MELTED HOUSE-MADE BUTTER AND GAME REDUCTION

Prep Time 1 hour
Cooking Time 1 hour 30 minutes

1 kg+ (2 lb 4 oz+) whole pheasant or similar game bird or rabbit
2 tablespoons extra virgin olive oil, plus extra for drizzling
1 large carrot, diced
1 large celery stalk, diced
1 large onion, diced
4 garlic cloves, minced
5 g (¼ cup) rosemary leaves
6 sage leaves, 4 left whole and 2 finely chopped
6 stems wild thyme, 4 left whole and 2 picked
200 ml (generous ¾ cup) single (pure) cream
300 g (3 cups) finely grated Parmigiano Reggiano
1.2 kg (2 lb 10 oz) Fresh egg pasta dough, rolled into sheets no thicker than 1 mm (page 240)
1 egg, beaten, for egg wash
125 ml (½ cup) Cognac
50 ml (scant ¼ cup) red wine
1 bay leaf
3 juniper berries
400 ml (1½ cups) Chicken stock (page 236)
2 tablespoons salt
4 tablespoons House-made butter (page 243)
Sea salt and freshly ground black pepper

This is a classic Northern Italian dish that you will find outside the Veneto area, stretching from Piedmonte all the way across to Friuli, and it's one of my all-time favourite things to eat. Here we use pheasant, but any game product, including rabbit, venison, quail and wild boar, can be a substitute.

Preheat the oven to 180°C (350°F).

Season the pheasant thoroughly with salt and pepper. Heat the olive oil in a large frying pan for 2 minutes, then add the pheasant and brown all over.

Put the carrot, celery, onion, three-quarters of the garlic, the rosemary, 4 whole sage leaves and 4 wild thyme stems in a roasting tin. Drizzle with a little olive oil. Place the pheasant on top of the vegetables and herbs in the tin and roast in the oven for 45 minutes.

Strip the meat off the bird. Using a butcher's cleaver or large knife, cut the carcass (bones) into small pieces and set aside. Finely dice the meat from the bird, allow to cool, then refrigerate.

Mix the diced pheasant meat with the chopped sage and picked thyme, the cream and Parmigiano Reggiano. Adjust the seasoning if required.

To make the tortellini, cut the pasta into 5 cm (2 inch) circles and add a teaspoon of pheasant mix to the middle of each. Using a pastry brush, wet one side of each pasta circle with egg wash, then fold to form half moon shapes, then twist each side to the centre to form tortellini.

To make the game reduction, remove the whole sage leaves and thyme stems from the roasting tin and reserve. Add the chopped pheasant carcass to the roasting tin and return to the oven. Cook for 20 minutes or until brown. Add the Cognac and a little of the red wine to deglaze the roasting tin.

Spoon all the ingredients from the roasting tin into a saucepan and add the reserved whole sage leaves and thyme stems. Add the rest of the red wine, the remaining garlic, bay leaf and juniper berries. Cook over low heat until reduced to a syrup consistency, then add the chicken stock and cook until reduced to a third of its volume. Pass through a fine sieve and season if required.

Bring a large pan of water to the boil and add 2 tablespoons salt. Cook the tortellini in the boiling water until they float. Melt the butter in a frying pan on the stovetop and toss the drained tortellini in the butter.

Serve the tortellini drizzled with melted butter and the game reduction.

—Serves 4

Mains

DRUNKEN SPATCHCOCK AND MOUNTAIN MUSHROOM FRICASSEE *with* RED CORN POLENTA

Prep Time 20 minutes, plus 24 hours marinating
Cooking Time 1 hour 20 minutes

4 spatchcocks
10 whole baby pearl
    onions, peeled
1 carrot, finely diced
1 celery stalk, finely diced
4 garlic cloves, finely diced
1 bottle Padovan 'Novello' red
    wine (or any light-style
    red wine)
125 ml (½ cup) Cognac
150 ml (generous ½ cup)
    extra virgin olive oil
1 litre (4 cups) Chicken stock
    (page 236)
100 g (3½ oz) fresh chanterelle
    mushrooms, sliced (or shimeji
    or portobello mushrooms)
2 sprigs rosemary
190 g (1 cup) red corn (Storo)
    polenta (or yellow polenta)
60 g (2 oz) Parmigiano Reggiano
100 g (3½ oz) butter
Sea salt and freshly ground
    black pepper
Fresh herbs, to garnish

This is a Padovan version of the iconic French dish, *coq au vin* – a beautiful wintery, indulgent dish for the family. It's essential that the spatchcock is marinated for 24 hours, allowing the flavours of the red wine and Cognac to seep into the meat, transferring a stunning and intense flavour.

Cut the spatchcocks into quarters (marylands and breasts), with the breasts left on the bone. Combine the spatchcock, vegetables, garlic, red wine and Cognac in a large bowl. Cover and refrigerate for 24 hours.

Remove from the refrigerator and strain. Pat dry the spatchcock and vegetables with paper towel, keeping the wine and Cognac.

Heat the oil in a large cooking pot or flameproof casserole dish for 2 minutes over medium heat. Add the spatchcock pieces, skin-side-down, and brown the skin. Turn and cook for 2 more minutes. Remove the spatchcock and set aside.

Add the strained onions, carrot, celery and garlic to the pot and cook for 4 minutes over medium heat, continually stirring. Add the red wine and Cognac and cook for 30 minutes, until reduced by half.

Preheat the oven to 180°C (350°F).

Return the spatchcock to the pot and season with salt and pepper. Add the chicken stock, mushrooms and rosemary and bring to the boil.

Transfer the pot to the oven and cook for 35–40 minutes. Taste and adjust the seasoning, if required.

Meanwhile, bring 1 litre (4 cups) water to the boil in a large pan and slowly add the polenta in a stream, stirring continuously. Cook, stirring, for 40 minutes. Add the cheese and butter and season with salt. Mix thoroughly, then cover the pan with a lid and leave for 5 minutes.

Spoon the soft polenta onto a serving plate and add the spatchcock, vegetables and sauce. Garnish with any fresh herbs.

—Serves 4

ROASTED BASSANO TROUT, HOUSE-MADE BUTTER AND SAGE *with* BORLOTTI BEAN AND POTATO PURÉE

Prep Time 20 minutes, plus overnight soaking of the borlotti beans
Cooking Time 1 hour 10 minutes

200 g (1 cup) dried borlotti beans
375 ml (1½ cups) Bassano extra virgin olive oil (or any quality extra virgin olive oil), plus extra for the fish
1 French shallot, finely diced
2 garlic cloves, finely diced
20 g (1 cup) sage leaves
600 g (1 lb 5 oz) quality mashing potatoes
150 ml (generous ½ cup) Buttermilk (page 243)
100 ml (scant ½ cup) single (pure) cream
4 whole plate-size trout
100 g (3½ oz) House-made butter (page 243)
Juice of 1 lemon
Sage flowers or any edible flowers or herbs, to garnish
Sea salt and freshly ground black pepper

This dish hails from Bassano, and celebrates the region's remarkable local river trout, made all the more enjoyable with home-made butter. It's worth the effort to make your own, and it's not nearly as daunting as some think. Don't let the process distract you from the cooking of the fish though. One of my all-time favourite things to eat is whole fish, cooked on the bone. Take care, however, as it quickly loses its appeal when overcooked.

Place the dried borlotti beans in a saucepan and add 2.5 litres (10 cups) of water. Bring to the boil and cook for 3 minutes. Remove from the heat, allow to cool, drain and then cover with fresh water. Leave in the refrigerator overnight.

Drain and rinse the beans.

Pour 125 ml (½ cup) of the oil into a saucepan and heat on the stovetop. Add the French shallot, garlic and a third of the sage and gently sauté until the French shallot and garlic are translucent. Do not season.

Add the borlotti beans and just cover with cold water.

Bring to the boil, then turn the heat down to a simmer. Cover the pan and cook for 45 minutes until the beans are tender. Transfer to a blender or food processor and blend to a purée.

Meanwhile, wash, peel and quarter the potatoes. Put them in a large pan and cover with cold water. Add ½ tablespoon salt and cook over medium heat for 20–25 minutes or until soft. Drain the potatoes. Note that you want to time the beans and potatoes to finish cooking at the same time, so the potatoes need to start cooking about 20 minutes after the beans.

Heat the buttermilk, cream and 200 ml (generous ¾ cup) of the olive oil in another small pan. Bring up to high heat but do not allow to boil. Add the buttermilk mixture to the hot drained potatoes and mix with a wooden spoon. Push the potato mixer through a ricer and then a sieve into a large bowl. Add the borlotti bean purée and mix together.

Preheat the oven to 200°C (400°F).

To make the roasted Bassano river trout, score across the fillets of the whole fish with a sharp knife, making about five incisions 1 cm (½ inch) deep on each side of the fish.

Rub the trout outside and inside the scoring cuts and inside the cavity with 70 g (2½ oz) of the butter, ensuring the fish have a generous covering. Season with sea salt and ground black pepper to taste. Place a sage leaf in each of the score incisions and then place two additional sage leaves in the cavity of each fish.

Put the remaining butter and oil on a baking tray and heat in the oven until the butter starts to bubble.

Arrange the trout on the hot tray and roast in the oven for 6 minutes. Turn the fish over and roast for another 4–5 minutes, taking care not to overcook the fish in the hot oven. Remember that the fish will continue to cook after it is taken out of the oven – the goal is to have the fish just cooked and with a crispy, buttery skin.

Remove the trout and deglaze the tray with the lemon juice. Serve the trout on a bed of the potato and borlotti bean purée and pour the pan juices over the top of the fish. Garnish with sage flowers, or any edible flowers or herbs.

—Serves 4

SPIT-ROASTED VICENZA GUINEA FOWL
with POMEGRANATE AND WILD HERB MISTICANZA SALAD

Prep Time 20 minutes
Cooking Time 1 hour

2 pomegranates
1 kg (2 lb 4 oz) whole guinea
    fowl (or chicken or
    game birds, including
    duck or pheasant –
    cooking times may vary)
5 g (¼ cup) sage leaves
100 g (3½ oz) House-made butter,
    softened (page 243)
1 lemon
1 whole head of garlic
100 ml (scant ½ cup) extra
    virgin olive oil
Sea salt and freshly ground
    black pepper

Misticanza salad
900 g (8 cups) mixed salad leaves,
    herbs and edible flowers
Juice of 1 lemon
Juice of 1 orange
100 ml (scant ½ cup) Agrumato
    lemon extra virgin olive oil

In Vicenza this recipe is often made with baby turkey in place of guinea fowl, and it's a common sight on dining tables at family feasts throughout the Christmas season. The spit-roasting process – the best for roasting meats – provides short bursts of intense heat. Because the meat is being cooked on the bone, you end up with the most succulent, flavourful result.

To prepare the pomegranates, cut each in half and hold one half over a bowl, cut-side-down. Using a wooden spoon in the other hand, tap the skin side of the fruit and the seeds will fall out into the bowl. Remove any white pith from the seeds.

Reserve half of the pomegranate seeds for the salad. Crush the remaining seeds with a potato masher to obtain the juice and then strain through a fine strainer.

To prepare the guinea fowl, use your fingers to carefully separate the skin from the flesh on the breasts and make a pocket. Place half the sage leaves and the softened butter under the skin and season with salt and pepper.

Cut the lemon and head of garlic in half and place in the body cavity of the bird with the remaining sage. Season with salt and pepper. Rub the outside of the bird with the olive oil and season with salt and pepper.

Put the bird onto a spit skewer and secure, then place onto a preheated spit rotisserie over high heat and set as close to the flame as possible. Cook for 40–60 minutes, basting the bird with pomegranate juice about every 10 minutes.

Alternatively, you can roast the bird in an oven. Preheat the oven to 200°C (400°F). Place the bird in a roasting tin and roast for 15 minutes, then lower the oven to 180°C (350°F) and roast for a further 35–45 minutes, basting every 10 minutes, until the juices run clear when you pierce the thigh with a knife.

When the bird is cooked, remove from the spit or oven, cover with foil and leave in a warm place for 20 minutes.

To make the misticanza salad, wash and dry the salad leaves. Pick the leaves from the herbs and toss with the salad leaves and edible flowers.

Mix the lemon juice, orange juice and lemon olive oil and season with sea salt and pepper. Toss the salad leaves, herbs, edible flowers and pomegranate seeds with the lemon and orange dressing.

Carve the guinea fowl into four portions, drizzle with the remaining pomegranate juice and serve with the misticanza salad.

Note
Guinea fowl is a specialty game bird that can be difficult to source. Specialty butchers might be able to order them in, even if they don't regularly stock them.

—*Serves 4*

VERONESE BEEF AND CHERRY PASTISSADA
with CELERIAC AND PANCETTA GRATIN

Prep Time 30 minutes
Cooking Time 3 hours

Beef and cherry pastissada
4 tablespoons extra virgin olive oil
1 kg (2 lb 4 oz) boneless beef shin
350 ml (1⅓ cups) Valpolicella
    DOC red wine (or any
    medium-bodied red wine)
1 litre (4 cups) Beef stock
    (page 237)
2 garlic cloves, minced
1 bay leaf
1 cinnamon quill
2 teaspoons mustard powder
Juice of 1 orange
Juice of 1 lemon
1 teaspoon raw sugar
1 teaspoon freshly ground
    black pepper
600 g (1 lb 5 oz) ripe fresh
    (Veronese) cherries, pitted
1 tablespoon butter
Sea salt and freshly ground
    black pepper

Celeriac and pancetta gratin
1 kg (2 lb 4 oz) celeriac, peeled
    and cut into 4–5 mm
    (¼ inch) thick slices
50 g (2 oz) butter, plus extra
    for brushing
100 g (3½ oz) rolled pancetta,
    thinly sliced and diced into
    5 mm (¼ inch) pieces
1 onion, finely diced
1 garlic clove, finely diced
100 g (3½ oz) Parmigiano
    Reggiano, grated

The traditional version of this dish, by which my recipe is inspired, is *pastissada de caval*. It was, and still is, made traditionally with horse meat. This is the most important dish of Verona, a region where equine butchers are more prevalent than conventional butchers. This recipe is a more modern version, using beef as the meat and fresh cherries from the Veronese hills. It's served with a wonderful gratin of pancetta and celeriac – the latter being almost exclusively cultivated in the province of Verona, to the point where it is often referred to as 'the celery of Verona'.

Preheat the oven to 170°C (325°F).

To make the pastissada, heat a deep flameproof casserole dish over high heat. Add the oil and heat for 2 minutes, then add the beef shin and brown on all sides.

Add the red wine and cook until almost evaporated. Add the beef stock, garlic, bay leaf, cinnamon, mustard powder, orange and lemon juice, raw sugar and pepper and stir thoroughly. Put the lid on the casserole and transfer to the oven. Cook for 2 hours, turning frequently.

Add the cherries to the casserole, cover and cook for a further 30 minutes.

Meanwhile, to make the gratin, bring a pan of water to the boil, add the celeriac and blanch for 2 minutes, then drain.

Heat the butter in a sauté pan over low heat and cook the pancetta, onion and garlic until the onion has softened and is fully cooked.

Divide the Parmigiano Reggiano in half, keeping half for the top of the dish.

Arrange a layer of celeriac neatly over the base of a baking dish, brush with butter and season with salt and pepper. Scatter with a little pancetta, onion and garlic mix and then grated Parmigiano. Repeat the layers until you have used all the ingredients, finishing with a layer of Parmigiano.

Remove the beef casserole from the oven, turn the temperature to 200°C (400°F) and bake the gratin for 20 minutes until golden brown.

Strain the liquid from the casserole into a pan and simmer over low heat on the stovetop until it has reduced and thickened to a sauce consistency. Reheat the beef and cherries in the sauce and then lift out onto plates. Whisk the butter into the sauce just before serving, and spoon over the meat and cherries. Serve with the gratin.

—Serves 4

'LESSO' VERONESE COTECHINO SAUSAGE AND MIXED CUTS *with* PEARA AND CREN SALSAS

Prep Time 30 minutes (the salsa cren to be prepared 2 weeks in advance)
Cooking Time 3 hours 30 minutes

1 onion, chopped into large pieces
2 carrots, chopped into
large pieces
4 celery stalks, chopped into
large pieces
2 bay leaves
10 peppercorns
1 veal shank
300 g (10½ oz) pork belly,
bone-in
400 g (14 oz) cotechino sausage
½ capon/boiling chicken

Salsa cren
400 g (14 oz) horseradish
40 g (scant ¼ cup) sugar
2 teaspoons salt
500 ml (2 cups) white
wine vinegar

Salsa peara
100 g (3½ oz) bone marrow
50 g (2 oz) butter
250–500 ml (1–2 cups) Beef
or Veal stock (page 237)
65 g (1 cup) dried breadcrumbs
Whole peppercorns, to taste
50 g (2 oz) Parmigiano Reggiano,
grated (optional)
Sea salt and freshly ground
black pepper

Known as *lesso* or *bollito misto*, this is another example of classic Northern Italian winter fare and is a personal favourite of mine. The Veronese version utilises particular condiments, including *cren* (freshly grated horseradish in salt and a little sugar) and *peara* (a bone marrow and bread sauce with black pepper). The quantity of black pepper is a subject of great conjecture and is completely at the discretion of the cook. With pepper being one of my favourite ingredients, I say be generous!

To make the *salsa cren*, grate the horseradish into a mixing bowl, then stir in the sugar and salt. Place in an airtight sterilised jar, then pour the white wine vinegar over to cover. Seal the jar and leave for 2 weeks to marinate.

Place the onion, carrot, celery, bay leaves, peppercorns, veal shank, pork belly and cotechino sausage into a large stockpot and cover with 4 litres (16 cups) water. Bring to the boil, then lower the heat to a simmer and cook for 1 hour, skimming off the excess fat from the top of the liquid throughout this cooking time. The cotechino will be quite salty, so check the cooking liquid after 30 minutes to see if it requires further seasoning (it shouldn't).

After 1 hour, lift out the cotechino and place in a bowl with enough poaching liquid to cover it. Cook the meats and vegetables in the stockpot for a further 1 hour.

Add the capon to the stockpot and add more water if needed to cover the meats. Check the seasoning again and simmer again for 1 hour.

Return the cotechino to the stockpot, bring to the boil, then reduce the heat and simmer for a further 20 minutes.

To make the *salsa peara*, place a small pan over low heat. Add the bone marrow and butter and allow to melt. Pour in the stock, stirring continuously, then mix in the breadcrumbs. Cook slowly for at least 1½ hours. Season with ground pepper, whole peppercorns and sea salt: the amount of pepper used is personal preference. Freshly grated Parmesan is also a great addition to *salsa peara*.

Slice the meat and serve with the vegetables and two salsas as condiments.

Notes
This recipe is really another version of nutrient-rich bone broth, often used to cook vegetables and legumes such as lentils. To increase the nutritional value of this dish, the braising liquid can be replaced with unseasoned beef bone stock.

The *cren* recipe will make a lot more than is required here. Store the remainder in an airtight container in the fridge: it will keep for a long time and can be used whenever horseradish is called for. It's beautiful served with steak or oily fish, such as salmon and trout.

—*Serves 4*

VEAL CHEEKS *with* MILK RISOTTO CAKES, SAVOY CABBAGE AND CHESTNUTS

Prep Time 20 minutes, plus 1 hour for chilling the risotto cakes
Cooking Time 4 hours 30 minutes

4 veal cheeks (250 g/9 oz each), cleaned of excess fat (or beef cheeks)
150 ml (generous ½ cup) extra virgin olive oil
1 carrot, diced
1 celery stalk, diced
2 onions, diced
4 garlic cloves, sliced
1 tablespoon tomato paste (concentrated purée)
300 ml (1¼ cups) Euganean Chardonnay DOP (or any good chardonnay)
700 ml (scant 3 cups) Beef, Veal or Chicken stock (page 236–7)
2 sprigs rosemary
2 bay leaves
Sea salt and freshly ground black pepper

Milk risotto cakes
1.2 litres (5 cups) milk
160 g (¾ cup) Vialone Nano rice (or any risotto rice)
60 g (2 oz) Parmigiano Reggiano, grated
70 g (2½ oz) butter
1 egg, lightly beaten
Extra virgin olive oil, for cooking

Savoy cabbage and chestnuts
250 g (9 oz) raw whole chestnuts
¼ whole savoy cabbage
175 g (6 oz) butter
150 g (5½ oz) rolled pancetta, diced
Olive oil, for cooking

In the Veneto, *risotto latte* was always considered *cucina povera,* or food of the poor. The milk risotto was a breakfast staple for many working-class Italians and its simplicity made it the perfect comfort food. Like a lot of 'poor people's' food, it tastes fantastic. I've given it a modern makeover here, converting it into risotto cakes and serving them with an absolutely stunning product (if you can get your hands on it): veal cheeks. If you don't have any luck at the butcher, beef cheeks make a great substitute.

Preheat the oven to 160°C (315°F).

Season the veal with salt and pepper.

Heat half the olive oil in a flameproof casserole dish over medium heat for 3 minutes, then add the veal cheeks and brown all over for about 3–4 minutes. Remove and set aside.

Add the carrot, celery and onion to the dish and cook for 5 minutes or until the vegetables become translucent. Add the garlic and tomato paste and cook again for 2 minutes.

Return the veal cheeks to the dish and cover with wine and stock. Add the rosemary and bay leaves and cover. Place in the oven and cook for 3½–4 hours until the veal is very tender and comes apart with the pressure of a fork.

Meanwhile, prepare the milk risotto cakes and cabbage.

To make the milk risotto cakes, pour the milk into a saucepan and season with salt and pepper. Bring to a simmer over medium heat, stirring continuously with a flat-bottomed wooden spoon.

Add the rice and cook for 15 minutes. The milk should slowly bubble through the cooking process and the rice and milk should slowly thicken. Stir continuously to avoid the milk and rice sticking to the bottom of the pan and burning.

When the rice is cooked, add the Parmigiano and 20 g (¾ oz) of the butter and stir to thoroughly combine. Cover the pan and set aside to cool, then refrigerate for at least 1 hour.

Mix the egg into the cold milk risotto. Use your hands to roll into balls of about 80 g (3 oz) each: the recipe should make about 8 balls. Press the balls gently to flatten them to about half their height. Place on a baking tray and cover with a tea towel.

To make the savoy cabbage, place the chestnuts in a saucepan and cover with water. Bring to a gentle boil and cook for 20 minutes or until they are soft in the centre. Set the chestnuts aside to cool. When cool enough to handle, peel off the outer shells.

Cut the cabbage into quarters, remove the core and cut into 2 cm (¾ inch) strips.

Melt 75 g (2½ oz) of the butter in a saucepan over medium heat. Add the pancetta and cook until crisp, then season with salt and pepper. Add the cabbage and allow to fully wilt, then cook for a further 2–3 minutes.

To cook the risotto cakes, place a small non-stick pan over medium–high heat and add the remaining 50 g (2 oz) butter and a little olive oil. When the butter begins to foam, add the risotto cakes and cook for 2–3 minutes or until golden brown and crispy. Flip and repeat on the other side, ensuring the cakes are hot in the centre.

In another pan, add another 50 g (2 oz) butter and a little olive oil and cook the chestnuts until they caramelise and are golden in colour, then season.

Once the veal is cooked, remove from the casserole dish and cover. Strain the cooking liquid into another saucepan and simmer over low heat until reduced to the consistency of a light sauce.

Return the veal cheeks to the sauce to heat through before serving. Serve with the risotto cakes, cabbage and caramelised chestnuts and veal sauce.

—*Serves 4*

Dolci

VENETIAN CARNIVAL FRITTERS

Prep Time 10 minutes, plus 1 hour soaking
Cooking Time 10 minutes

250 g (1½ cups) sultanas
4 egg yolks
500 g (3⅓ cups) 00 flour,
    plus extra for dusting
2 teaspoons baking powder
400 g (1¾ cups) caster sugar
100 ml (scant ½ cup) rum
Juice and zest of 1 orange
Zest of 1 lemon
175 ml (¾ cup) vegetable oil
175 ml (¾ cup) milk
4 tablespoons egg whites
2 litres (8 cups) grapeseed
    oil, for frying

You will find these in the *pasticcerie* throughout the whole of the Veneto during the annual *Carnevale* period – a time of particular indulgence and excess every January. This version is fantastic, but an equally beautiful iteration is made without sultanas and with a custard centre. These are best served warm with an espresso (and good luck stopping at one).

Soak the sultanas in warm water for 1 hour, drain and dry on paper towels, then dust with a little flour to absorb any excess moisture.

In a large mixing bowl, mix together the egg yolks, flour, baking powder and half the caster sugar. Add the rum, orange juice and zest, lemon zest, vegetable oil, milk and sultanas and beat until smooth.

Whisk the egg whites until stiff, then fold through the batter.

Heat the grapeseed oil in deep pan or deep fryer to 180°C (350°F).

Using a tablespoon, spoon the batter into the hot oil and cook for 2–3 minutes until brown. Turn and cook for 2–3 minutes on the other side.

Remove the fritters from the oil and roll in the remaining caster sugar to serve.

—Serves 8

PANDORO TIRAMISU *with* HOME-MADE MASCARPONE

Prep Time 10 minutes, plus overnight refrigeration, if desired

4 egg yolks
2 tablespoons caster sugar
2 egg whites
450 g (2 cups) Mascarpone
    (page 243)
500 ml (2 cups) strong
    black coffee
100 ml (scant ½ cup) Marsala
½ pandoro
3 tablespoons dark cocoa powder

Pandoro is Veronese Italian Christmas cake and is a variation of the famous panettone, which literally translates to 'big bread', thanks to its filling of raisins and peel. Pandoro, or 'bread of gold', differs as it has no peel or raisins in the mix. Here I use it in an unusual way as part of another classic Italian dessert that hails from the Veneto's Treviso region: tiramisu.

Whisk the egg yolks and sugar in a large mixing bowl until pale and creamy.

Whisk the egg whites in a separate bowl until stiff.

Mix the mascarpone into the egg yolk mixture. Fold in half the egg whites and then fold in the remaining egg whites.

Combine the coffee and Marsala.

Slice the pandoro into 2 cm (¾ inch) thick slices.

You will need a 23 cm (9 inch) x 10 cm (4 inch) deep glass bowl. Lay half the pandoro slices over the base of the bowl. Drizzle half the coffee over the pandoro. Pour half the mascarpone mixture over the top.

Repeat the layers, using up all the ingredients, then dust with cocoa.

This can be served immediately but, for best results, refrigerate overnight first.

—Serves 4

VALPOLICELLA SPICED PEARS *with* SWEET CREAM

Prep Time 30 minutes
Cooking Time 1 hour

4 pears
1 bottle Valpolicella DOC red wine (or any good-quality medium-bodied red wine)
75 g (⅓ cup) brown sugar
1 cinnamon quill
4 black peppercorns
2 cloves
Juice of 1 orange
Zest of ½ orange
1 sprig rosemary
1 vanilla pod
4 tablespoons pistachio nuts, roasted and chopped

Sweet cream
115 g (½ cup) Mascarpone (page 243)
125 ml (½ cup) thick (double) cream
Zest of ½ lemon
2 tablespoons icing (confectioners') sugar

This is a simple, yet stunning, dessert. It showcases one of Italy's most revered wine appellations, Valpolicella, where vine cultivation is said to be traced back to the fifth century BC. Produced in the Veneto, Valpolicella is one of the most beloved red wines in Italy, recognised for its rich black cherry and cranberry aromas and soft tannins. And while it makes for exceptional drinking, it's very commonly cooked with in and around Venice, including in her national dish of slow-cooked beef stew, *pastissada*, as well as in a number of desserts.

Peel the pears and slice in half lengthways, then remove the cores with a melon baller or small teaspoon, keeping the stalks intact for presentation.

Combine the red wine, brown sugar, cinnamon, peppercorns, cloves, orange juice, orange zest and rosemary in a saucepan.

Cut the vanilla pod in half lengthways and scrape out the seeds. Place the whole vanilla pod and half the seeds in the pan with the wine (keeping the remaining seeds for the sweet cream).

Place the saucepan over medium heat and bring to a simmer, then add the pears and cook for 1 hour until tender. Remove the pan from the heat and let the pears cool in the poaching liquid.

For the sweet cream, combine the mascarpone, cream, lemon zest, icing sugar and remaining vanilla bean seeds in a mixing bowl and whisk until the mixture is like lightly whipped cream.

Serve the pears either warm or chilled, with the sweet cream and garnished with the pistachio nuts and a little of the poaching liquid.

—*Serves 4*

WILD BERRIES IN RECIOTO BIANCO *with* GRAPPA MASCARPONE *and* SAVOIARDI BISCUITS

Prep Time 20 minutes (the biscuits are best baked 24 hours in advance)
Cooking Time 15 minutes

Savoiardi biscuits
160 g (5½ oz) egg whites
120 g (generous ½ cup)
    caster sugar
120 g (4 oz) egg yolks
120 g (generous ¾ cup) plain flour,
    sifted
2 tablespoons icing
    (confectioners') sugar
2 tablespoons white sugar

Poli Museo grappa mascarpone
1 vanilla pod
185 ml (¾ cup) thick
    (double) cream
2 tablespoons white sugar
1 tablespoon Poli Museo grappa
    (or any quality grappa)
185 g (¾ cup) Mascarpone
    (page 243)

Wild berries in Recioto Bianco
½ tablespoon Ligurian bee honey
    (or any quality honey)
125 ml (½ cup) Recioto Bianco
    white dessert wine (or
    any semi-sweet white
    dessert wine)
415 g (3 cups) mixed wild berries

Simplicity at its best, this dessert is also a great celebration of the Veneto region's wine and spirit industries. The Recioto Bianco is a sweet wine made from Garganega grapes, usually from an area called Soave, renowned for its eponymous wine. Another beautiful inclusion is the Poli Museo grappa, aged in barrels for 25 years: an absolutely stunning product that is a perfect companion to fresh mascarpone.

To make the savoiardi biscuits, preheat the oven to 190°C (375°F).

Whisk the egg whites with half the caster sugar until stiff peaks form.

In another bowl, beat the egg yolks with the remaining caster sugar for 5 minutes until a pale cream colour.

Fold half the egg white into the egg yolk. Fold in the flour. Fold the remaining egg white into the egg yolk mixture.

Line a baking tray with baking paper and dust with icing sugar. Place the batter into a piping bag and pipe finger shapes onto the tray. (Use a purpose cast baking tray if you have one.)

Sprinkle the finger biscuits with the white sugar and bake for 7 minutes.

To make the Poli Museo grappa mascarpone, cut the vanilla pod in half lengthways and scrape out the seeds. Place half the seeds in a mixing bowl (keeping the pod and remaining seeds for the wild berries in Recioto Bianco). Add the cream and white sugar to the bowl and whisk until lightly whipped.

Mix together the grappa and mascarpone, add to the bowl and fold in.

To make the wild berries in Recioto Bianco, heat the honey slowly in a small saucepan over low heat with the remaining vanilla seeds and vanilla pod. Gently stir until the honey becomes a thin liquid. Pour in the wine and gently stir with a wooden spoon until completely mixed. Set aside and allow to cool.

continued...

Wash and prepare the berries by removing the stalks and cutting the large berries in half. Gently pat the berries dry and place in a mixing bowl.

Spoon 4 tablespoons of the Recioto Bianco and honey sauce into the bowl with the berries, mixing carefully so that the sauce covers all the berries. A little more sauce can be poured over the berries when serving.

Serve in glass coupes by spooning a little of the Poli Museo mascarpone cream into the bottom of the coupes first. Divide the berries evenly amongst the coupes, then add a little more of the mascarpone cream. Serve with one of the savoiardi biscuits to finish.

Notes
For best results, bake the savoiardi biscuits a day in advance and keep in an airtight container.

The Recioto and honey recipe will make more than this recipe requires, but this sauce will keep for a long time in an airtight container in the fridge.

—Serves 4

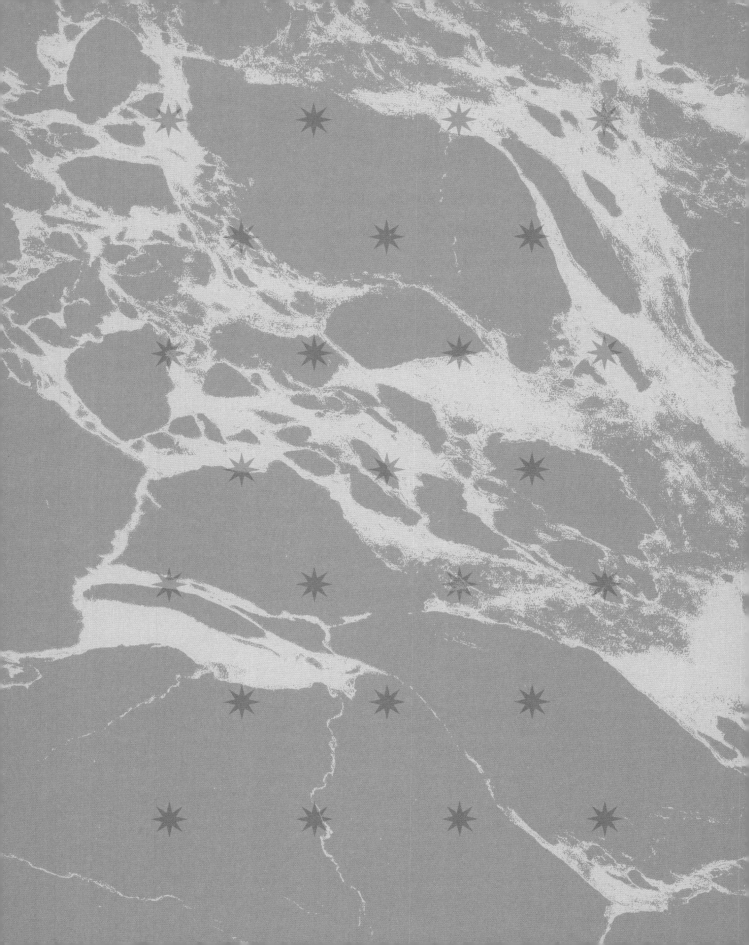

VENETIAN CROATIA

III

A MARITIME SUPERHIGHWAY

Simply put, without secure passage and control through the waters in and around the Croatian coast, Venice wouldn't have become what she did.

Spanning a great length of the Adriatic Sea, the Croatian coastline was a significant component of the footprint the Venetians needed to cross in order to trade with the East. Sitting between Venice and her key historical trading territories – particularly Greece and the Levant – it linked the Republic with some of her greatest wealth-generating products: cotton, wheat, spices, silk and the ash used for glass making (today an unrivalled industry in Venice). So, this region was critical.

The Croatian coastline and islands were the first lands claimed as part of the Republic's international expansion, and they were an absolutely essential win. Not only did this allow the Venetians to maintain their trading monopoly by removing competitive industries on the Croatian coast, the area also provided Venetians with the manpower, money and resources necessary for the next leg of their journey. And the Venetians were more than comfortable here. Like Venice, the Croatian coast is an archipelago, so Venice's boats would weave and wind through these stunningly beautiful island waterways, taking advantage of the ports along the way to pick up resources to either trade or take back home.

Venice ruled the Croatian coast for about 700 years, ending in the late 18th century. Although the Croatians are clearly and proudly their own people, distinctively independent with their own long and unique history, Venice's legacy can still very much be seen. Walk around the islands and the coast today and the winged lion – the symbol of the Venetian Republic – is scattered throughout, perched on top of the city gate of Zadar, the City Lodge of Loggia on Hvar and on the clock tower in Rovinj, known to this day as Croatia's 'Little Venice'.

VENETIAN REPUBLIC

Croatia had an impact on Venice too and the intercultural exchange traversed all sorts of things, not least of which was the bounty from its land and sea. Learned Venetians today will tell you that the famous Venetian dish of *scampi alla busara* is actually Istrian in origin. As is Istrian stone, or *pietra d'Istria*, the most prevalent stone in Venetian architecture, some of which proudly adorns the iconic ruler's (Doge's) palace in the Piazza San Marco.

Out of everything, however, food is where the Venetian influence is most visible. For me, eating on these islands and along the coast feels like eating in Italy. And how stunningly masterful they are at cooking this way, for if the Venetians brought influential recipes and culinary ideas, the Croatians have clearly shown that they understand them and have made them their own. Like with quality regional Italian cooking, it's usually pretty simple, but in the main, it's some of the best food in the world.

As you move inland, the influence becomes noticeably more Slavic. The food of the coast and islands, however, is indisputably Venetian influenced. They eat pasta and risotto like Venetians and Northern Italians do. Fish and seafood dominate and are often treated almost identically to how they are in Venice. Squid ink risotto, sweet pea risotto, the seafood stew known as *brodet* (*brodetto* in Italian), traditionally served over polenta, and beautifully simple pasta with truffles are national dishes seen absolutely everywhere along the Croatian coast. Close your eyes and taste the food: it's different, but you really could be in Italy. And it's not just what they eat; it's how they eat too. A meal on the Croatian coast typically comprises an antipasto (often locally made gently smoked charcuterie), then a pasta or risotto as an entrée, a main course and, to conclude, something sweet. Sound familiar? Without question, this is an Italian scheme of eating.

Travel south to Greece and its islands and it all changes quite dramatically. As you'll see in this book's final chapter, whilst much of Greece is heavily influenced by the Venetians, Greeks don't really eat like the Italians. Croatians do.

While seafood dominates the cuisine of the Croatian coast, it is a curious fact that it's a meat dish that coastal Croatia is most proud of; *pašticada*. Venetian influence? Of course. *Pašticada* is believed to have first originated in the Veneto – Verona, in fact – where in 489 AD the Goth king, Theodoric, won sovereignty for the city by overcoming barbarian enemies in an epic battle that saw a significant horse mortality rate. After the battle, the horse carcasses were given to the community and butchered, then the meat mixed with wine and aromatics before slow cooking. *Pašticada de caval* was born.

While horsemeat is still widely consumed in the Veneto today, most commonly in *pastissada de caval,* the use of beef in the dish *pastissada de manzo* is far more common in Venice, and is very similar to the *pašticada* of Croatia. Continue down the Adriatic and you'll find similar *pastissada*-inspired dishes; for example *pastitsada* in Corfu, the Greek island that also played a key role in the administration and defence of the Venetian Republic's critical trade routes. While each of these iterations has its own nuances, most share at least a few of the following key aromatics: pepper, cinnamon, cloves, bay leaves and nutmeg, which, as you now know, were riches acquired by the Venetians from the East.

Some of my absolute favourite recipes from this book reside in this chapter. Some of my favourite recipes of all time, in fact. Stunning food from a stunning place.

VENETIAN CROATIA

Antipasti

DALMATIAN WOOD-GRILLED CALAMARI
with RED PEPPER MAYONNAISE, PARSLEY AND ONION SALAD

Prep Time 20 minutes, plus 4 hours for marinating the calamari
Cooking Time 20 minutes

Wood-grilled calamari
500 g (1 lb 2 oz) calamari
125 ml (½ cup) quality early-
    harvest extra virgin olive oil
2 garlic cloves, sliced

Red pepper mayonnaise
4 whole red capsicums (peppers)
50 g (scant ¼ cup) Mayonnaise
    (page 241)
Sea salt and freshly ground
    black pepper

Parsley and onion salad
40 g (2 cups) Italian parsley leaves
65 g (½ cup) finely sliced
    red onion
4 tablespoons extra virgin
    olive oil
4 tablespoons lemon juice

This dish is a wonderful example of classic Dalmatian cooking, in which calamari is almost always grilled over coals or wood. Having said that, a barbecue or chargrill will deliver a similar result. For this recipe, it's important to use an early-harvest, high-quality olive oil, which the new wave of boutique producers along the Dalmatian coast are making lots of nowadays. The herbaceousness and intensity of this style of oil work beautifully with the chariness of the calamari.

To make the wood-grilled calamari, clean the calamari by removing the tentacles from the body and, with a knife, remove the hard beak from the centre of the head and reserve. With your fingers, pull the back bone, ink sac and intestines out of the body, then peel the outer membrane/skin from the calamari and wash under cold running water.

Lay the calamari tubes on a chopping board and score with a sharp knife at 2 cm (¾ inch) intervals. Turn the tubes over and repeat.

Place the calamari, including the reserved tentacles, in a bowl with the olive oil and garlic and marinate for 4 hours.

To make the red pepper mayonnaise, place the capsicums on a preheated grill or barbecue over high heat and cook on all sides until the outer skin turns completely black. Place in a bowl, cover with plastic wrap and leave to cool. Scrape off the blackened skin, cut the capsicums in half and remove the stalk and seeds. Do not wash with water or you will wash away the flavour.

Using a food processor, blend the mayonnaise and capsicums and season with salt and pepper.

Remove the calamari from the marinade and drain well. Season with salt and pepper and cook on a preheated grill or barbecue over high heat for 1 minute. Turn over and cook again for 1 minute. Transfer to a serving plate.

To make the parsley and onion salad, toss together the parsley leaves, red onion, oil and lemon juice. Season with salt and pepper and toss again.

Scatter the salad over the calamari and serve with red pepper mayonnaise.

—*Serves 6*

VENETIAN CROATIA ✳ *Antipasti*

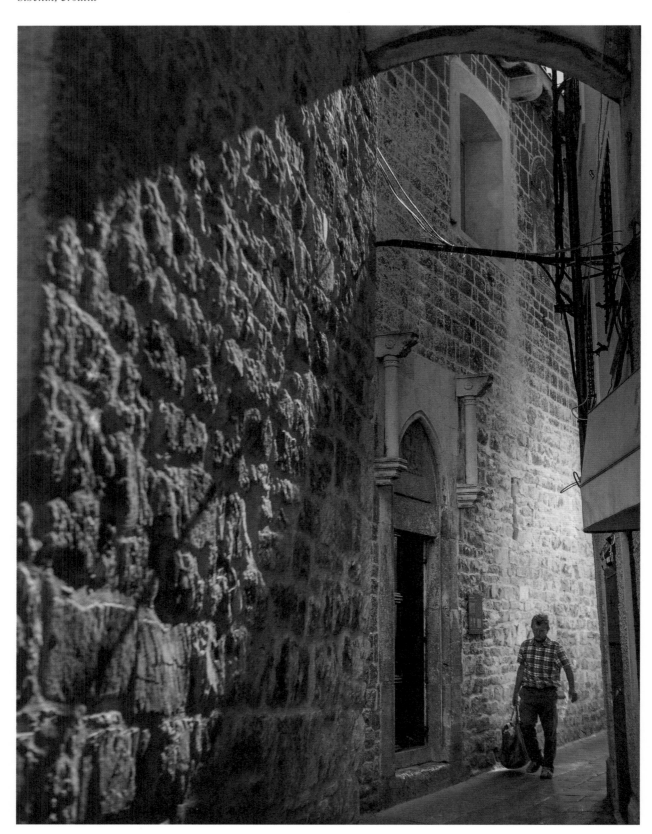

SIBENIK SALT COD FRITTERS
with SWEET-AND-SOUR VEGETABLES

Prep Time 30 minutes, plus 48 hours for soaking salt cod and marinating vegetables
Cooking Time 3 hours 10 minutes

Sweet-and-sour vegetables
2 tablespoons extra virgin olive oil
230 g (2 cups) finely diced
    vegetables: French
    shallots, celery, capsicum
    (pepper) and carrot
150 ml (generous ½ cup)
    white wine vinegar
100 g (½ cup) caster sugar
1 bay leaf
4 black peppercorns

Salt cod fritters
250 g (9 oz) *baccala* (salt cod)
1 onion, roughly chopped
Milk, to cover the cod
400 g (14 oz) potatoes, unpeeled
2 garlic cloves, minced
1 teaspoon baking powder
10 g (½ cup) parsley, chopped
1 egg
100 g (⅔ cup) plain flour
500 ml (2 cups) quality
    vegetable or olive oil, for frying
Sea salt and freshly ground
    black pepper

This is a dish inspired by an amazing meal I had at the Michelin-starred restaurant, Pelegrini, in Sibenik, arguably Croatia's best. Salt cod is commonly eaten in this part of the world, as it is throughout the rest of the Venetian Republic's territories. Traditionally served as *cicchetti* (snacks) in a whipped form on crostini or in sandwiches, these little bites are another great option for *aperitivo*, with the sourness of the vegetables contrasting beautifully with the fritters.

To make the sweet-and-sour vegetables, place a large frying pan over medium heat, add the olive oil and heat for 1 minute. Add the diced vegetables and sauté for 1 minute. Transfer the vegetables to a bowl.

Place the vinegar, sugar, bay leaf and peppercorns in a small pan and bring to the boil, then pour over the diced vegetables. Leave the vegetables to marinate for at least 24 hours before serving.

To make the salt cod fritters, wash the excess salt from the cod and then soak it in cold water in the fridge for 48 hours, changing the water twice each day. This will remove most of the fish's saltiness. After 48 hours, remove the fish from the water, discard the skin and pat dry with paper towels.

Place the cod and onion in a saucepan, cover with milk and simmer over medium heat for 3 hours. Leave until cool enough to handle, then remove all the salt cod flesh from the bone and discard the onion.

Meanwhile, place the potatoes in a large saucepan, cover with cold water and cook over low heat until tender. When the potatoes are cool enough to handle, remove the skins and coarsely mash with a potato ricer.

Combine the cooked potatoes, cod, garlic, baking powder, parsley and egg in a bowl and season with salt and pepper. Sift in the flour and mix through evenly.

Beat the mixture well, then form into small 20 g (¾ oz) balls and refrigerate for 2 hours to set.

Heat the vegetable oil in a deep pan over medium heat to 180°C (350°F).

In small batches, fry the cod fritters for roughly 3–4 minutes until golden brown, then remove and drain on paper towels.

To serve, place the marinated vegetables on a plate and top with the hot fritters.

—*Serves 4*

VENETIAN CROATIA ✳ *Antipasti*

DALMATIAN PAN-FRIED SARDINES
with WILD HERBS AND LEMON

Prep Time 10 minutes
Cooking Time 15 minutes

150 g (1 cup) plain flour
1 tablespoon lemon zest
12 sardines, scaled, gutted
    and cleaned
375 ml (1½ cups) olive oil
5 g (½ cup) wild dill
8 g (½ cup) wild
    marjoram leaves
5 g (½ cup) wild fennel fronds
    (or fennel herb fronds or bulb
    fennel tops)
8 g (½ cup) wild oregano
50 ml (scant ¼ cup) lemon juice
150 ml (generous ½ cup) premium
    Istrian extra virgin olive oil
    (or any quality extra virgin
    olive oil)
1 lemon, cut into wedges
Sea salt and freshly ground
    black pepper

One of my most treasured memories is being at my Zia Angela's house in the hills just out of Toulon, France, eating freshly delivered sardines on the back of the local fish vendor's *camion* (truck). I was in my early 20s and ever since I've absolutely loved sardines. This is a wonderfully simple dish that you will find all over the Mediterranean, and the Croatians do it as beautifully as anyone, including my aunty. If you find small enough sardines, eat them whole; if they're larger, once served, cut off the head and the back bone will come out easily.

Mix the flour, sea salt, black pepper and lemon zest in a large mixing bowl.

Place the sardines in the seasoned flour and coat lightly.

Pour approximately 1 cm (½ inch) olive oil into a large frying pan. Place over medium heat for 2 minutes, then add the sardines and cook for 2 minutes on each side.

Pick the leaves off the herbs and toss in a large bowl with the lemon juice, extra virgin olive oil and a pinch of sea salt.

Place the sardines on a serving platter and scatter the herb salad over the top. Serve with lemon wedges.

—Serves 4

DALMATIAN SMOKED PROSCIUTTO *with* PAG SHEEP'S MILK CHEESE, BLACK OLIVES AND GHERKINS

Prep Time 10 minutes

160 g (5½ oz) Pag sheep's milk
   cheese (or Tuscan or
   Sardinian pecorino)
12 thin slices premium
   smoked prosciutto
70 g (½ cup) dried black olives
60 g (½ cup) savoury pickled
   baby cucumbers (gherkins)
Crusty wood-fired bread, sliced
2 tablespoons extra virgin
   olive oil (optional)

Pag cheese – a hard, distinctively flavoured, sheep's milk cheese – is made on the Croatian island of the same name. It is one of the best pecorinos I've ever tasted and it marries wonderfully with Dris prosciutto, which is made distinctively Dalmatian by the fact that it's smoked. As well as a lovely smoky flavour, for this recipe you want prosciutto with a heavy marbling score. The additional fat content makes a big difference here and is offset beautifully by the acidity of the gherkins.

Crumble the cheese into large triangles.

Serve the cheese, prosciutto, olives and gherkins on a platter with crusty wood-fired bread. Drizzle extra virgin olive oil over the top, if desired.

—Serves 4

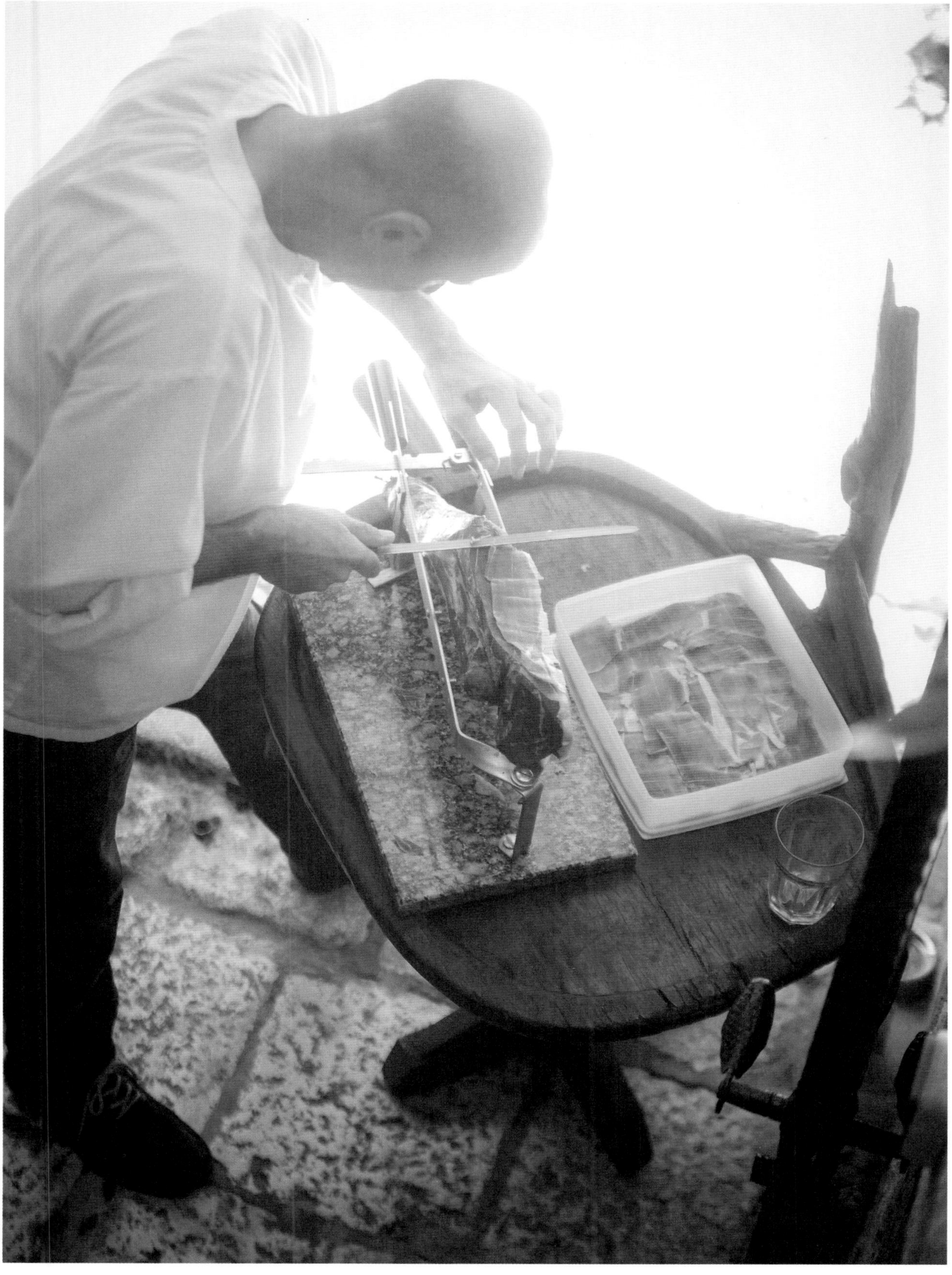

Pasta, rice and pies

CLASSIC SQUID INK RISOTTO *with* GRILLED BOTTLE SQUID

Prep Time 15 minutes
Cooking Time 30 minutes

600 g (1 lb 5 oz) bottle squid, left whole (or small whole calamari)
170 ml (⅔ cup) extra virgin olive oil, plus extra for drizzling
2 white onions, finely diced
3 garlic cloves, crushed
350 g (1⅔ cups) Vialone Nano (or any risotto rice)
125 ml (½ cup) white wine
2 tomatoes, chopped
50 g (2 oz) butter, softened
3 tablespoons squid ink
60 g (1 cup) chopped parsley
1 litre (4 cups) Fish stock (page 236)
Sea salt and freshly ground black pepper

After *pašticada*, squid ink risotto could easily take the title of Croatia's national dish and – unsurprisingly – it has a similar reputation in Venice. While the fisherman of the coast and local cooks in Croatia are adept at removing ink sacs from cuttlefish, if you want to avoid the jarred product (which is a suitable alternative), it will require quite a bit of skill and effort – and more than likely, a decent clean up. Either way, only work with super-fresh squid or cuttlefish.

Clean the squid by removing the head from the body, cut the beak out of the centre of the head, reserve the head and tentacles, pull the spine, intestines and ink sac carefully out of the body, then remove the wings and outer skin.

Heat the olive oil in a saucepan over low heat. Add the onion and garlic and cook until the onion is translucent.

Add the rice and cook for 2 minutes, then add 200 g (7 oz) of the squid. Add the wine and tomatoes and cook for 2 minutes over high heat. Stir in the butter, then stir in the squid ink and parsley.

Meanwhile, bring the stock to the boil in another pan, then reduce the heat and keep at a simmer.

Slowly add the hot fish stock to the rice, one ladle at a time, stirring continuously as the rice absorbs the stock. Cook for about 15–20 minutes until the rice is al dente. Season with salt and pepper.

Heat a cast-iron skillet over high heat until extremely hot, then sear the remaining squid tubes and tentacles quickly on both sides. Season with salt and pepper.

Spoon the risotto onto serving plates and top with the seared squid and a little more extra virgin olive oil, to taste.

—*Serves 4*

SWEET PEA RISOTTO

Prep Time 15 minutes
Cooking Time 30 minutes

160 g (5½ oz) smoked pancetta
80 ml (⅓ cup) extra virgin olive
  oil, plus extra for drizzling
2 white onions, finely diced
2 garlic cloves, sliced
350 g (1⅔ cups) Vialone Nano (or
  any risotto rice)
250 ml (1 cup) Istrian Malvasia
  white wine (or any quality dry
  white wine)
1 litre (4 cups) Vegetable or
  Chicken stock (page 236–7)
300 g (10 oz) sweet peas, half
  left whole, half puréed to
  a smooth paste
30 g (½ cup) chopped parsley
2 tablespoons butter
50 g (½ cup) grated Parmigiano
  Reggiano, plus extra to serve
Sea salt and freshly ground
  white pepper

This is one of Venice's most iconic dishes. But, as with *pašticada* and squid ink risotto, *rizi bizi* or sweet pea risotto, it is also ubiquitous in Croatia. This recipe includes a unique Dalmatian component: crisp smoked pancetta laid over the top, delivering a beautiful salty, smoky crunch.

Preheat the oven to 180°C (350°F).

Finely dice half the pancetta and cut the remainder into thin ribbons. Place the ribbon slices on a baking tray and cook in the oven until crisp.

Heat the olive oil in a saucepan. Add the onion, garlic and diced pancetta and cook over low heat until the onion is translucent.

Add the rice to the pan and cook, stirring, for 2 minutes. Increase the heat to high, add the wine and cook for 2 minutes or until the wine has evaporated.

Meanwhile, bring the stock to the boil in another pan, then reduce the heat and keep at a simmer.

Slowly add the hot stock to the rice, one ladle at a time, stirring continuously as the rice absorbs the stock. Cook for about 12 minutes, then stir in the peas, pea purée and parsley.

Cook for a further 3 minutes, then add the butter and Parmigiano Reggiano and season with salt and pepper. Stir well and leave for 3 minutes before serving, garnished with crisp pancetta slices, a little extra Parmigiano Reggiano and a drizzle of extra virgin olive oil.

—*Serves 4*

DALMATIAN PASTA AND BORLOTTI BEANS
with SMOKED PORK HOCK AND OLIVE OIL

Prep Time 30 minutes, plus overnight refrigeration of the beans
Cooking Time 1 hour 10 minutes

400 g (2 cups) dried borlotti beans
125 ml (½ cup) extra virgin olive oil, plus extra for drizzling
150 g (5½ oz) smoked pancetta, diced into 5 mm (¼ inch) square pieces
70 g (½ cup) diced celery
80 g (½ cup) diced carrot
80 g (½ cup) finely diced onion
3 garlic cloves, crushed
1 teaspoon chopped thyme
2 potatoes, diced
200 g (7 oz) smoked ham hock/smoked pork ribs
2 litres (8 cups) Chicken stock (page 236)
150 g (5½ oz) dried short pasta (macaroni)
30 g (½ cup) chopped parsley
Sea salt and freshly ground black pepper
Grated Pag cheese (or Parmigiano Reggiano), to serve

Known locally as *pasta fazol*, this is similar to the Italian version, *pasta e fagioli*, meaning pasta and beans, found not only in Venice but throughout the whole of Italy. It's a very classic Italian dish. This version is slightly different, but equally fantastic. I love the smokiness of the hock/ribs as well as the pancetta – ingredients and flavours well and truly mastered along the Dalmatian coast.

Place the borlotti beans in a saucepan, cover with water and bring to the boil. Boil for 3 minutes, then cool, drain and cover with fresh water. Refrigerate the beans overnight.

Heat the oil in a large deep saucepan over medium heat for 1 minute. Add the pancetta, celery, carrot, onion, garlic and thyme and cook for 5 minutes, stirring continuously.

Add the drained beans, potato, ham hock and stock and bring to the boil, then turn down the heat and cook for 1 hour, or until the beans are tender.

Take the hock out of the pan and remove the meat from the bone. Shred and return the meat to the pan along with the pasta. Cook over medium heat until the pasta is cooked. Stir in the parsley and season to taste.

Serve in pasta bowls, drizzled with olive oil and with grated Pag cheese, to taste.

—*Serves 10*

GNOCCHI *with* ISTRIAN PORCINI MUSHROOMS *and* PAG CHEESE

Prep Time 30 minutes
Cooking Time 30 minutes

Gnocchi
500 g (1 lb 2 oz) whole, unpeeled
    floury potatoes
1 egg, lightly beaten
40 g (scant ½ cup) grated
    Parmigiano Reggiano
40 g (1½ oz) salted butter,
    softened and diced
½ teaspoon sea salt
100 g (⅔ cup) plain flour

Sauce
125 ml (½ cup) extra virgin
    olive oil
320 g (11½ oz) fresh
    porcini mushrooms, sliced
½ tablespoon finely
    chopped thyme
125 ml (½ cup) white wine
20 g (⅓ cup) chopped parsley
Sea salt and freshly ground
    black pepper
4 tablespoons grated Pag cheese
    (or any quality Tuscan or
    Sardinian pecorino), to serve

This recipe – that of my dear Croatian friend and fellow chef, Ino Kuvacic, – utilises two of my favourite ingredients: amazing porcini mushrooms, in this case grown in Istria (which borders Italy), and Pag cheese. The latter can be substituted with parmesan or a mild pecorino. Regardless of which cheese you choose, ensure it's of a reasonable age so it can impart a beautiful, strong flavour to the finished dish. And, as with all gnocchi, moisture is your enemy here. Be sure to use very starchy potatoes, and remove as much water from them as possible after boiling by patting with tea towels. This will significantly reduce your reliance on flour, therefore guaranteeing lovely, light and pillowy home-made gnocchi.

To make the gnocchi, place the potatoes in a large pan of cold water and cook over medium heat until tender.

Drain and peel the potatoes while still hot. Using a food mill or mouli, purée the potatoes into a large bowl. Add the egg, Parmigiano Reggiano, butter and sea salt, then carefully work in the flour to form a dough.

Dust a work surface with a little flour to prevent the dough sticking, then divide the dough into quarters. Roll each one into a log, then cut into 2 cm (¾ inch) pieces. Using a spatula, place the gnocchi on a tray lined with baking paper and refrigerate until needed.

To make the sauce, heat the oil in a large sauté pan over medium heat for 1 minute. Add the porcini mushrooms and thyme and sauté until the mushrooms have softened.

Add the white wine and parsley, increase the heat to high and cook for 2 minutes, then season with salt and pepper.

Bring a pan of water to the boil, add the gnocchi and cook until they rise to the surface. Drain the gnocchi, toss with the porcini sauce, and season with salt and pepper.

Finely grate the Pag cheese over the top of the gnocchi to serve.

—Serves 4

PLJUKANCI PASTA *with* PORK AND GRAŠEVINA RAGU, ZADAR PROSCIUTTO *and* BLACK TRUFFLES

Prep Time 40 minutes
Cooking Time 1 hour 40 minutes

400 g (14 oz) Fresh egg
   pasta dough (page 240)
4 tablespoons extra virgin
   olive oil
600 g (1 lb 5 oz) minced pork
   (30% fat)
1 onion, finely sliced
80 g (½ cup) finely diced carrot
70 g (½ cup) finely diced celery
4 garlic cloves, chopped
250 ml (1 cup) Graševina white
   wine (or any good-quality dry
   white wine)
500 ml (2 cups) Chicken stock
   (page 236)
1 tablespoon chopped rosemary
2 bay leaves
6 thin slices Zadar prosciutto
   (or any high-quality prosciutto)
40 g (1½ oz) Zadar black truffle
   (or any black truffle)
Pag cheese or Parmigiano
   Reggiano, to serve (optional)
Sea salt and freshly ground
   black pepper

Making use of local truffles from Rovijn, this dish is very similar to what's served throughout Northern Italy but, once again, has the distinctive smoky aroma and taste of local prosciutto. Pljukanci, a hand-rolled, spindle-shaped pasta that hails from the Croatian region of Istria, is easier to make than you'd think, and an absolute joy to eat.

Take small, nut-sized pieces of pasta dough and roll between the palms of your hands to create long, thin noodles, similar in size to green beans, but thinner at the ends. Place the pasta on a lightly floured tray.

Heat half the olive oil in a pan over high heat for 2 minutes, then add the pork mince and cook until browned. Remove the pork from the pan and set aside.

Add the remaining olive oil to the pan, add the onion, carrot, celery and garlic and cook over low heat until the onion is translucent.

Return the pork, with any juices, to the pan, add the white wine and cook over high heat for 2 minutes.

Add the chicken stock, rosemary and bay leaves to the pan and cook over low heat for 90 minutes.

Cut the prosciutto into thin strips and fold through the pork ragu. Season with salt and pepper.

Place the pasta into a large pan of boiling salted water and cook for just 2 minutes. Drain the pasta and toss through the pork ragu.

Shave or grate the truffle over the top of the pasta before serving. You can also add grated Pag or Parmigiano, if desired.

—*Serves 6*

VENETIAN CROATIA ✳ *Pasta, rice and pies*

SPINACH AND NETTLE RISOTTO *with* SEA SCALLOPS

Prep Time 30 minutes
Cooking Time 45 minutes

100 g (3½ oz) stinging nettles
   (or spinach)
100 g (3½ oz) spinach
70 ml (⅓ cup) olive oil
1 onion, finely diced
350 g (1⅔ cups) Vialone Nano
   rice (or any risotto rice)
125 ml (½ cup) white wine
1.5 litres (6 cups) Vegetable or
   Chicken stock (page 236–7)
100 g (3½ oz) butter
12 half-shell scallops
1 garlic clove, minced
Sea salt and freshly ground
   black pepper

The visual wow factor here is thanks to the vibrant green of the nettles, best picked in early spring. Of course, you don't need to serve the scallops in their shells, but they not only add to the dish's aesthetic appeal, they also allow the scallops – which should be only just caramelised on both sides – to sit in the beautiful garlic butter.

Wear food prep gloves to prepare the stinging nettles. Pick the nettle leaves from their stalks and place in a bowl of cold water.

Bring a large pot of salted water to the boil. Place the nettles and spinach in the boiling water for approximately 30 seconds until just wilted. Remove from the water and place in a bowl of ice water to stop the cooking process.

Drain the spinach and nettles and squeeze to remove any water. Process in a food processor to a smooth purée, adding a little cold water or stock, if required.

Heat the olive oil in a saucepan, add the onion and cook over low heat until translucent. Add the rice and cook for 2 minutes, stirring continuously. Add the white wine and cook for 2 minutes.

Meanwhile, bring the stock to the boil in another pan, then reduce the heat and keep at a simmer.

Slowly add the hot stock to the rice, one ladle at a time, stirring continuously as the rice absorbs the stock. Cook for about 15–20 minutes. Season with salt and pepper

Fold the spinach and nettle purée into the risotto. Add half the butter and season, then stir through the risotto. Cover and set aside to rest.

Remove the scallop meat from the shells, reserving 4 shells for serving. Heat the 4 presentation shells in the oven, in boiling water or under a grill.

Place a cast-iron skillet over high heat until extremely hot and sear the scallops on each side for 10 seconds. Season with salt and pepper.

Remove the scallops from the pan and add the garlic. Cook for up to 20 seconds until the garlic starts to turn golden, then add the remaining butter. Remove the pan from the heat and allow the butter to melt.

Place the risotto in serving bowls and add one scallop shell to each. Arrange three scallops in each shell. Spoon the melted butter and garlic over the scallops.

Note
Stinging nettles can be sourced from produce markets or gourmet food stores.

—Serves 4

Mains

WHOLE FLOUNDER AND HERB BREADCRUMBS
with CROATIAN SAMPHIRE

Prep Time 15 minutes
Cooking Time 1 hour

Roast potatoes
400 g (14 oz) potatoes
200 ml (generous ¾ cup)
    extra virgin olive oil
5 g (¼ cup) chopped rosemary
Sea salt and freshly ground
    black pepper

Flounder with herb crust
60 g (1 cup) fresh sourdough
    breadcrumbs
1 heaped teaspoon lemon zest
Juice of 1 lemon
10 g (¼ cup) parsley leaves
1 kg (2 lb 4 oz) whole flounder,
    cleaned and scaled
Extra virgin olive oil, to drizzle
1 lemon, cut into quarters

Croatian samphire (*motar***)**
80 g (1 cup) picked samphire
    (or any sea succulent)
1 tablespoon lemon juice
3 tablespoons extra virgin olive oil

Samphire is a sea succulent that's becoming more and more popular in the UK and Europe, particularly in the Mediterranean and along the Dalmatian coast, where it's known as *motar*. It might be hard to track down, but it's worth the effort: it adds a lovely fresh, salty element to the fish, and matches perfectly with the potatoes (make sure you get them crispy) and the fish's herb crust.

Preheat the oven to 180°C (350°F).

To make the roast potatoes, finely slice the potatoes 5 mm (¼ inch) thick and toss in the extra virgin olive oil. Add the chopped rosemary and season.

Layer the potatoes, overlapping slightly, to cover the base of a large ovenproof dish. Roast in the oven for 25 minutes, until browned and crisp. Remove and cover with foil. Increase the oven to 200°C (400°F).

To make the flounder with herb crust, place the breadcrumbs, lemon zest, lemon juice and parsley in a food processor and blend until the crumbs become bright green. Season with salt and pepper.

Season the flounder with salt and pepper on each side and in the internal cavity. Place on a greaseproof paper-lined baking tray and drizzle with extra virgin olive oil. Lightly and evenly cover the flounder with the herb crust.

Bake the flounder for 25–30 minutes or until just cooked. Just before the fish is ready, return the potatoes to the oven to reheat.

Meanwhile, to make the Croatian samphire, place the samphire in a pan of boiling salted water for 20 seconds, then drain and toss with the lemon juice and extra virgin olive oil. Season with sea salt and pepper.

Serve the flounder with the roasted potatoes, samphire and lemon quarters.

—Serves 4

CLASSIC DALMATIAN COAST SEAFOOD GRILL

Prep Time 20 minutes
Cooking Time 1 hour 45 minutes

300 g (10½ oz) octopus
500 g (1 lb 2 oz) whole
    snapper, cleaned and scaled
4 large whole prawns, cut
    in half and left in shell
4 scampi/langoustines, cut in half
    and left in shell
250 ml (1 cup) extra virgin olive
    oil, plus extra for the lemon
    and to drizzle
1 lemon, cut in half
Wild herbs, to garnish
Sea salt and freshly ground
    black pepper

This is a classic example of Mediterranean cooking and can be found all along the Dalmatian coast in a form that's basically identical to what is seen in Venice. What I most love about this dish is how it allows the quality of the seafood to speak for itself. In Croatia this dish usually includes a whole fish and, in fact, there's often more than one different type. Croatians understand that eating fish on the bone really is the best way to enjoy seafood, and I couldn't agree more.

With a heavy meat mallet or rolling pin, beat the octopus for about 20 seconds to tenderise.

Place the octopus into a pot of salted boiling water. When the water comes back to the boil, turn the heat down to medium and cook for 90 minutes. Remove from the heat and leave to cool in the cooking liquid. Drain the octopus and cut into individual tentacles.

Preheat a chargrill or barbecue to medium heat.

Lightly coat the seafood with olive oil and season with salt and pepper. Place the snapper on the grill and cook on each side for approximately 6–8 minutes (the cooking time varies with the size of fish and the heat of the grill).

Five minutes before the snapper is ready, add the octopus, turning after 2 minutes. Add the prawns and scampi: these will take about 2 minutes to cook.

Brush the cut side of each lemon half with olive oil and grill until caramelised.

Serve the grilled seafood on a platter with the lemon and drizzle with extra virgin olive oil. Garnish with any wild herbs.

—Serves 4

DUBROVNIK TUNA PAŠTICADA
with YELLOW POLENTA *and* SMOKED EGGPLANT

Prep Time 15 minutes
Cooking Time 45 minutes

Red wine sauce
100 ml (scant ½ cup) extra
 virgin olive oil
310 g (2 cups) finely diced onion
4 garlic cloves, crushed
300 ml (1¼ cups) Plavac
 Mali red wine (or Primitivo
 or Zinfandel)
50 ml (scant ¼ cup) Prošek
 sweet wine (or any quality
 white dessert wine)
50 g (2 oz) dates, diced

Grilled polenta
1 teaspoon sea salt
125g (⅔ cup) fine yellow polenta
60 g (generous ½ cup) finely
 grated Parmigiano Reggiano

Smoked eggplant
1 eggplant (aubergine)
20 g (⅓ cup) shredded parsley
4 tablespoons extra virgin olive oil
1 tablespoon red wine vinegar
1 garlic clove, finely diced
Sea salt and freshly ground
 black pepper

Tuna steak
640 g (1 lb 7 oz) tuna loin, cut
 into 4 steaks
2 tablespoons olive oil

This is quite a modern interpretation of *pašticada*, which as I've said is one of Croatia's national dishes. And, while it's clearly different to Venice's version, which showcases beef, the two key similarities are the red wine – in this case Croatia's celebrated Plavac Mali – and the inclusion of polenta, used in various forms and guises throughout the region, but which should be nice and crispy here.

To make the red wine sauce, heat the olive oil and onion in a saucepan over low heat and cook, stirring continuously, until the onion is translucent. Add the garlic and cook for 2 minutes.

Add both the wines to the pan and cook until reduced to a third of the original volume. Stir in the dates and set aside to cool.

To make the polenta, place 500 ml (2 cups) water and the salt into a saucepan and bring to the boil. Pour the polenta into the water in a slow, steady stream, stirring continuously. Turn the heat to low and cook, stirring, for 20 minutes.

Stir the Parmigiano Reggiano into the polenta. Pour the polenta into a small greased baking tray and leave to cool: the polenta should be approximately 3 cm (1¼ inches) thick. When cool, cut the polenta into 5 cm (2 inch) squares.

To make the smoked eggplant, cook the eggplant over high heat on a preheated grill or barbecue until the skin is completely charred all over. Put the eggplant in a bowl, cover with plastic wrap and leave to cool.

When cool enough to handle, carefully cut the eggplant in half and scoop out the flesh with a spoon. Place the eggplant flesh in a clean bowl and fold in the parsley, olive oil, red wine vinegar, garlic, salt and pepper.

Preheat a grill pan or cast-iron skillet to high heat.

Lightly brush the tuna steaks with olive oil and season on both sides. Cook the tuna and polenta squares on the grill for 2 minutes on each side.

Arrange the polenta on serving plates and top with smoked eggplant and the tuna steaks. Spoon the red wine sauce over the fish before serving.

—Serves 4

VENETIAN CROATIA ✳ *Mains*

ISTRIAN MIXED SHELLFISH BUZARU

Prep Time 15 minutes
Cooking Time 20 minutes

200 ml (generous ¾ cup) Istrian
extra virgin olive oil (or any
quality extra virgin olive oil),
plus extra for drizzling
4 tablespoons fresh breadcrumbs
4 garlic cloves, finely chopped
350 g (12 oz) peeled prawns
350 g (12 oz) lobster tail, shell
on, cut into 4 escalope pieces
350 g (12 oz) whole scampi/
langoustines
350 g (12 oz) venus clams
375 ml (1½ cups) Malvasia white
wine (or any quality medium–
dry white wine)
140 g (5 oz) quality tomato
passata (puréed tomatoes)
1 tablespoon chopped parsley
Crusty bread, to serve
Sea salt and freshly ground
black pepper

Known throughout the Croatian coast as *buzaru*, the classic version of this dish calls only for scampi, served in a simple but delightful tomato sauce. The recipe is also common in Venice and the Veneto, but it's usually accompanied by pasta – primarily spaghetti. Both versions are absolutely delicious, but I have to say I love this recipe, with its wider range of fish and shellfish.

Heat 100 ml (scant ½ cup) extra virgin olive oil in a small frying pan over medium heat for 1 minute, then add the breadcrumbs and fry until golden brown. Drain on paper towels.

Heat the remaining olive oil in a saucepan, add the garlic and cook gently over low heat for 2 minutes, taking care not to brown. Add the shellfish and wine and cook until the scampi and lobster start to become pink.

Add the tomato passata and cook for 5 minutes until the sauce thickens. Season with salt and pepper and stir in the parsley.

Serve on a deep platter, sprinkled with the fried breadcrumbs and drizzled with a little extra virgin olive, to taste. Serve with crusty bread.

—Serves 4

BRAISED PAG LAMB SHOULDER *with* OLIVE OIL MASHED POTATOES *and* GRILLED BABY LEEKS

Prep Time 10 minutes
Cooking Time 4 hours 15 minutes

Lamb shoulder
1.2 kg (2 lb 10 oz) whole
    shankless lamb shoulder
2 tablespoons olive oil
120 g (1 cup) whole
    French shallots
5 garlic cloves, crushed
1 bottle Plavac Mali red wine
    (or Zinfandel, Primitivo or
    any medium/full-bodied
    red wine)
125 ml (½ cup) red wine vinegar
1 sprig thyme
1 sprig rosemary
2 bay leaves
Sea salt and freshly ground
    black pepper

Olive oil mashed potatoes
800 g (1 lb 12 oz) potatoes, whole
    and unpeeled
200 ml (generous ¾ cup) olive oil

Grilled baby leeks
20 baby leeks
3 tablespoons extra virgin olive oil

The wonderful Croatian island of Pag, best known for its eponymous sheep's milk cheese, also (and unsurprisingly) produces absolutely stunning lamb. This is a great winter's dish, with the meat falling off the bone and packing a flavourful punch, thanks to both the hint of acidity from the vinegar and the richness of the Plavac Mali, the superstar red wine of the Croatian islands.

Preheat the oven to 160°C (315°F).

Season the lamb shoulder well with salt and pepper.

Heat the olive oil in a large, deep flameproof casserole dish over high heat for 2 minutes. Carefully add the lamb shoulder and brown all over. Remove the lamb and set aside.

Turn the heat to low, add the shallots and garlic and cook until softened.

Return the lamb to the dish and cover with the red wine and vinegar. Add the thyme, rosemary and bay leaves. Cover the casserole and cook in the oven for 3½ hours or until the lamb is very tender.

Remove the lamb and cover with foil in a warm place. Strain the liquid through a sieve and return the cooking juices to a saucepan over low heat. Simmer the liquid until it reduces to a sauce consistency, then keep warm.

Meanwhile, to make the olive oil mashed potatoes, place the potatoes in a large deep pan of cold water and boil until cooked through. While still hot, peel the potatoes and purée in a food mill or mouli. Beat in the oil and season with salt.

To make the grilled baby leeks, trim the roots of the leeks, brush with olive oil and season with salt. Place on a hot grill and cook for 1 minute on each side.

Serve the lamb on a platter with the sauce, olive oil potato mash and baby leeks.

—Serves 4

SPIT-ROASTED FARM HEN AND WHITE ROVINJ TRUFFLE *with* POTATO AND RAINBOW CHARD

Prep Time 15 minutes
Cooking Time 1 hour

Spit-roasted farm hen
1 farm hen (or medium chicken)
150 g (5½ oz) butter, softened
4 tablespoons extra virgin olive oil
1 whole head of garlic
4 g (¼ cup) picked thyme
20 g (¾ oz) Rovinj truffle (or any white or black truffle – black truffles have a milder flavour)
Sea salt and freshly ground black pepper

Potato and rainbow chard
3 potatoes, peeled, cut into 2.5 cm (1 inch) dice
80 ml (⅓ cup) extra virgin olive oil
4 garlic cloves, finely sliced
1 bunch orange and red Swiss chard, cut into 2 cm (¾ inch) strips

Croatians enjoy cooking and eating meat and fish on the bone, and this dish is a stunning example. Spit-roasting the farm hen keeps the flesh lovely and moist, while also giving it a wonderfully caramelised skin. If you're not able to use a spit, oven roasting will work well too, although you might miss the lovely charry flavour that comes from cooking over a flame. For those who can find (and afford) such a luxury, the truffle makes a sensational addition, as does the potato and rainbow chard – a classic combination seen all over the Croatian coast.

For the spit-roasted farm hen, preheat the spit roast to a medium–high heat, or the oven to 180°C (350°F).

Starting at the neck end of the bird, use your finger to separate the skin from the flesh, pushing your hand between the skin and breast meat to form a cavity, then gently do the same to the thighs, making sure not to tear the skin.

Take the softened butter and place evenly in the cavity under the skin. Rub the olive oil all over the bird, then season with salt and pepper inside and outside. Cut the head of garlic in half and place inside the bird with the thyme. Place the bird onto the spit and secure according to the manufacturer's instructions.

Cook until the bird's internal temperature reaches 70°C (160°F) – this should take approximately 1 hour. Alternatively, roast in the oven for 50–60 minutes. Then cover with foil and leave to rest for 20 minutes.

Meanwhile, to make the potato and rainbow chard, put the potato in a pan of cold water and boil over high heat until tender but not falling apart. Drain.

Place a large frying pan over low heat, add the olive oil and garlic and cook for 2 minutes. Add the potatoes and cook for 3–4 minutes. Add the Swiss chard and cook until wilted. Season with salt and pepper.

Carve the bird with a sharp knife: remove the legs, then the breast meat, cut into even pieces and arrange on a serving platter.

Slice or grate the truffle over the bird and serve with potato and rainbow chard.

—Serves 4

Dolci

CROATIAN BLACKBERRY CRUMBLE

Prep Time 15 minutes
Cooking Time 50 minutes

Pastry
150 g (1 cup) plain flour
⅓ teaspoon baking powder
170 g (6 oz) cold butter, diced
110 g (½ cup) caster sugar
2 egg yolks

Blackberry filling
2 egg whites
110 g (½ cup) caster sugar
500 g (1 lb 2 oz) blackberries
Seeds from ½ vanilla pod
1 teaspoon lemon zest
1 tablespoon icing
    (confectioners') sugar

In many parts of the world, fruit crumble desserts like this one are reserved for the cold of winter. Not in this case, as blackberries are at their best in summer, and this Croatian staple – another example of Slavic influence on the Dalmatian coast – is beautifully light and fantastic for summer.

Preheat the oven to 180°C (350°F).

To make the pastry, mix the flour, baking powder, butter, sugar and egg yolks in a food processor until a dough ball forms. Turn out of the processor and set aside one-third of the dough to make the topping.

Grease a 20 cm (8 inch) pie dish and firmly press the dough into the base and side of the dish to form a crust.

For the blackberry filling, whisk the egg whites and sugar into soft peaks. Fold in the berries, vanilla seeds and lemon zest and pour into the pie dish.

Crumble the reserved pastry dough over the top of the blackberry filling.

Bake the crumble in the oven for about 50 minutes, or until golden.

Allow to cool a little, then dust with icing sugar. This is beautiful with vanilla bean gelato or cream.

—Serves 8

RAB ISLAND ALMOND AND MARASCHINO LIQUEUR CAKE

Prep Time 30 minutes, plus 1 hour for resting the dough
Cooking Time 50 minutes

Dough
130 g (scant 1 cup) 00 flour
1 egg, beaten
20 g (¾ oz) unsalted butter, softened
1 tablespoon caster sugar
1 pinch sea salt

Filling
200 g (2 cups) ground almonds
200 g (1⅔ cups) icing (confectioners') sugar, plus extra for dusting
1 egg
1 tablespoon maraschino cherry liqueur
Zest of 1 orange
Zest of 1 lemon

6 almonds

It's said that this cake was first served to Pope Alexander III in 1177 on the Croatian island of Rab, and it became a delicacy served to the aristocracy during the Venetian Republic's dynasty. Today, it's served at festive occasions, including baptisms and weddings, and is one of the island's most famous exports. And, while the traditional spiral shape is sometimes replaced with a heart or a horseshoe, it's considered almost sacrilegious in Rab's town to deviate from the classic recipe. Resembling more of a biscuit than a cake when cut, Rab cake is just beautiful served with coffee.

To make the dough, mix together the flour, egg and butter in a large bowl. Add 2½ tablespoons water, the sugar and salt and knead for 12 minutes to form a smooth, silky dough.

Divide the dough in half, cover with plastic wrap and leave to rest for 1 hour.

Preheat the oven to 120°C (235°F).

To make the filling, beat together the ground almonds, icing sugar, egg, liqueur, orange zest and lemon zest in a large bowl with a spatula.

Place half the dough on a floured work surface and, using a rolling pin, roll out to a 25 × 30 cm (10 × 12 inch) rectangle. Place on a tray lined with baking paper.

Using a pastry wheel, cut the dough into a tight spiral snake, 5 cm (2 inches) wide, then top the pastry spiral with the filling to cover all the pastry.

Roll out the other half of the pastry dough to the same thickness as the base, and cut into 2 cm (¾ inch) wide ribbons. Attach the ribbons of dough all the way around the edges of the spiral, pinching the dough together to seal.

Score the top of the cake filling with a fork to decorate, then press whole almonds into the top.

Bake for 50 minutes, or until the outside crust is firm. Just before serving, dust with icing sugar.

—*Serves 8*

APPLE AND CHERRY STRUDEL

Prep Time 10 minutes
Cooking Time 50 minutes

1 tablespoon honey
450 g (1 lb) cooking apples
1 tablespoon lemon zest
325 g (11½ oz) pitted fresh cherries
    (or 350 g/12 oz unpitted)
65 g (⅓ cup) soft brown sugar
¼ teaspoon fine sea salt
1 teaspoon ground cinnamon
150 g (1¼ cups) walnut halves
10 sheets filo pastry
100 g (3½ oz) butter, melted
2 tablespoons caster sugar

Like pancakes, strudels are ubiquitous in Croatia. Served in patisseries and a regular menu inclusion along the Dalmatian coast, strudels like this one are also seen in the northern parts of the Veneto, especially in the town of Belluno and further north near the Austrian and Slovenian borders. Cherries, a staple fruit in Croatia used in a range of desserts and liqueurs, are the star here, so make sure you find them at their peak.

Preheat the oven to 160°C (315°F).

Gently heat the honey in a pan over low heat until it becomes runny, like water.

Peel, core and dice the apples into 1 cm (½ inch) cubes. Combine in a large mixing bowl with the honey, lemon zest, cherries, brown sugar, sea salt, cinnamon and walnuts.

Brush each sheet of filo all over with melted butter and lay the sheets on top of each other. Spoon the apple and cherry filling lengthways onto the pastry, to about 4 cm (1½ inches) from each end of the pastry. Fold the pastry from one side and roll to form a log. Fold in the ends to seal in the filling and then brush the outside of the pastry with butter. Sprinkle with caster sugar.

Place the strudel on a baking tray and bake for 35–45 minutes.

Allow to cool for 20 minutes before slicing to serve.

—*Serves 10*

DUBROVNIK ROSE LIQUEUR, RICOTTA AND ALMOND CREPES *with* CANDIED ROSE PETALS

Prep Time 10 minutes, plus overnight drying of rose petals and 20 minutes for resting batter
Cooking Time 10 minutes

Candied rose petals
3 egg whites
20 g (1 cup) clean, unsprayed rose petals
110 g (½ cup) caster sugar

Crepe batter
150 g (1 cup) plain flour, sifted
1 egg, beaten
375 ml (1½ cups) milk
2 tablespoons butter

Ricotta filling
230 g (1 cup) ricotta
240 g (1 cup) Mascarpone (page 243)
30 g (¼ cup) icing (confectioners') sugar, plus extra for dusting
3 tablespoons Dubrovnik rose liqueur (or rose water)
160 g (1 cup) roasted blanched almonds, chopped

Pancakes and crepes are absolutely everywhere in Croatia and, in fact, are hugely popular throughout much of Europe. Less common is the combination of ingredients I've used here; however, each one is classically Croatian and they're stunning all together. This is a simple but beautiful treat for all the senses, with the candied rose petals adding a great visual element.

To make the candied rose petals, lightly whisk the egg whites to a frothy consistency, then lightly brush the rose petals with egg white. Dip into the caster sugar, then place the petals on a tray lined with baking paper. Place the tray of petals in a warm dry place to dry overnight.

To make the crepes, place the flour in a large mixing bowl and make a well in centre. Add the egg and a little milk and whisk to a smooth paste. Whisk in the remaining milk. Pass through a fine sieve and leave to rest for 20 minutes.

Heat a non-stick frying pan or crepe pan over medium heat and add ½ teaspoon of the butter. Add a small ladle of crepe batter to cover the base of the pan. Cook for 1 minute, turn over and cook again for 1 minute. Repeat with the remaining crepe batter.

To make the ricotta filling, whisk together the ricotta, mascarpone, icing sugar and rose liqueur until smooth. Fold in half the chopped almonds.

Place 3 tablespoons of ricotta filling on each crepe and spread evenly. Roll each crepe into a cigar shape.

Dust the crepes with icing sugar and serve with candied rose petals and the remaining chopped almonds.

—Serves 4

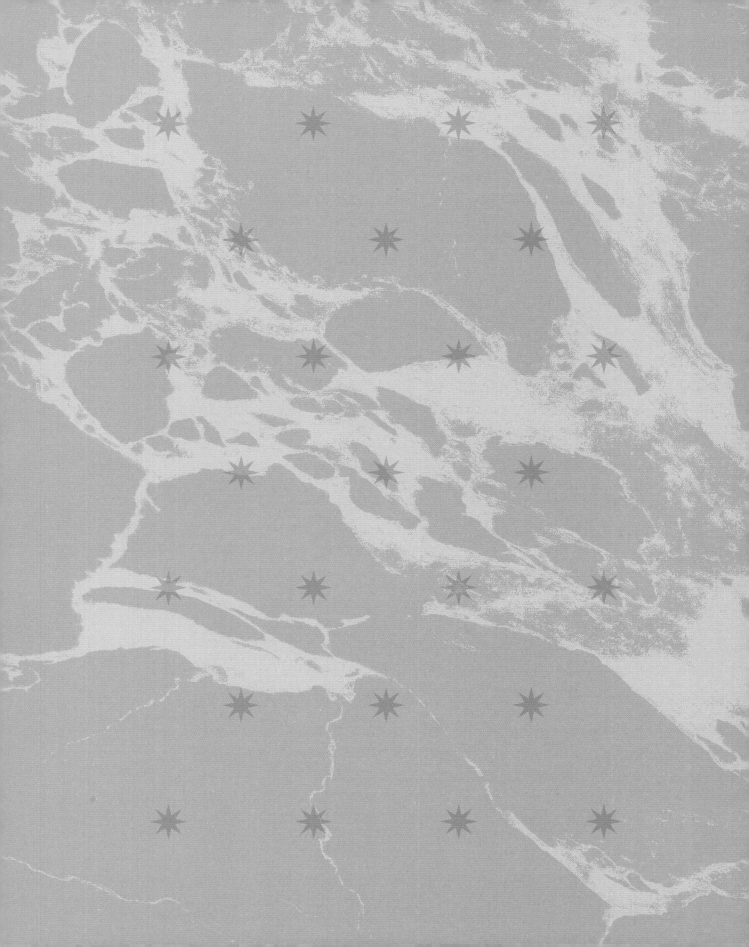

GREEK
ISLANDS
OF THE
REPUBLIC

IV

GATEWAY TO THE EAST

To this day, the people of the Greek lands formerly under Venetian rule often reflect nostalgically on this part of their history. Whilst foreign invasion was never going to be a harmonious event, Venetian rule brought stabilising benefits to this part of the world and its people. It meant protection from the East and frequently facilitated a livelihood supported by Venice's international trade of key Greek agricultural assets. For the most part, Venice's reign over her Greek territories was mutually beneficial, with many cultural blessings being shared between the two throughout the Republic's 450-odd year rule.

Corfu, with her strategic location and rich agricultural potential, was a significant coup, forming part of the Republic in 1386. It, and a multitude of islands and land-based ports in both the Ionian and Aegean Seas, formed Venice's key Greek outposts. Zante, Cephalonia, Ithaca, Lefkada and Kythera formed the Venetian-ruled Ionian islands: the only Greek-speaking territories (with the exception of Cephalonia for a very short period of time) that didn't succumb to Ottoman rule. Crete, Santorini and Cyprus were key Venetian-held islands in the Aegean.

Under Venetian rule, the islands' economies were primarily based on producing and exporting trading commodities. On Corfu, the most important agricultural product was olive oil. This was also the case on Cephalonia and Zante, along with raisins and wine. For Crete, it was grain, hides and wood for shipbuilding.

Occupying parts of Greece was extremely valuable to Venice. Just as with the Dalmatian coast, gaining control of the Greek island ports bolstered the Republic's trading capabilities in the East Mediterranean, which by the end of the 14th century had reached almost monopolistic status. Greece was the gateway between the East and West, and the authority that the Ottomans exerted on her mainland was matched by Venice in the water. Control of the Greek islands secured Venice's trading relationship with the Levant – with Crete and Cyprus of particular importance. This was key to Venice cementing her status as an economic powerhouse. And, as was the case with the Croatian coast, the Venetian raison d'etre and way of life was also ideally suited to these islands, with her boats very much at home in these waters.

Some Greeks profited enormously from this arrangement. The Greek aristocratic classes of the day, owners of large areas of Greek land, enjoyed the full fruits of these export markets. The arrangement also facilitated access to 'new' and 'exotic' foods introduced by Venetians from the Americas and Indies, including corn, tomatoes, beans and coffee, commodities that have since become synonymous with daily life in Greece.

The legacy of the Venetian Republic can still be seen on the islands today, where there are numerous and clear parallels between their cuisine and that of Venice. But what I also find fascinating are the linguistic similarities between the two regions – not all that surprising considering that despite Venice's rule ending in 1797, Italian was still the official language of the Ionian islands until well into the 1800s.

The correlations are perhaps most evident in Corfu, the closest island to Italy, a kind of Venice without canals. Their classic *bourdeto* is a spicy fish stew whose name, like the Croatians' *brodet*, hails from the Italian word *brodetto*, meaning 'broth'. Corfiot *pastitsada (*again like Croatia's *pašticada*) also closely resembles Venice's *pastissada*, a slow-cooked beef stew, but using rooster or veal as the primary ingredient. *Bianco*, the Italian word for 'white', is fish usually cooked in a lemon or white wine sauce with garlic (as it often is in Italy). A typical fish dish on many Greek islands is *savoro* – inarguably a direct relative of Venice's *in saor*. The language similarities extend beyond the culinary. The words *nonna* and *nonno* for 'grandmother' and 'grandfather' is a significant language difference between the Venetian-ruled territories and the rest of Greece, and a clear example of the longevity of Venice's impact in this part of the world. There are many other examples. Further, in Corfu, those with ethnic and linguistic ties to the Venetian Republic are still known as Corfiot Italians. During Venice's leadership, many Venetians moved to the Greek island, incentivised by free land. Today you'd struggle to find a more Venetian island outside of Italy. Likewise, Lefkada was settled by people from the Venetian island of Burano, who brought with them the age-old custom of charcuterie making, a custom for which Lefkada is famous to this day – and an artform noticeably absent elsewhere in Greece. Crete too was significant, and was the Republic's most important cultural centre outside of Venice through this period.

Symbols of Venice's influence are scattered across many of the Greek islands. The look and feel of Ithaca's capital, Vathi, is very Venetian – even to the point that after devastating earthquakes in 1953, the Venetian buildings were rebuilt in the exact same style and, in 1978, a law was passed prohibiting repairs in any other manner. Zakynthos boasts her own Piazza San Marco, albeit a small and less revered version of the Venetian original. In Cephalonia, the Assos Castle – now a popular tourist attraction – was built in the 16th century to fend off invasion. It's the work of Venetian architect Marino Gentilini, whose descendants remained on the island and now produce some of her most stunning wines, particularly the indigenous varieties, Robola and Mavrodaphne. And what does each bottle proudly display? A logo boasting none other than a Venetian lion. In Crete, the Venetian harbour of Chania was used to manage trade and fend off pirates, and together with her lighthouse (also built by the Venetians) is probably the island's most recognised setting. Finally, in the Republic's furthest flung territory, Cyprus' fortifications and bridges are present-day reminders of the island's role as a military base, enabling its trade with the Levant.

The following recipes provide an illuminating snapshot into the cuisine of these unique islands. The Venetian influence is apparent in most of the dishes, and I think it is some of Greece's best food.

GREEK ISLANDS OF THE REPUBLIC

Antipasti

IONIAN ISLAND BRUSCHETTE

In this recipe I've used sourdough baguette, but in Greece twice-cooked barley or wheat flour rusks are commonly used. If you'd like to do the same – and can find them – be sure to sprinkle the tops of the rusks with a little water. This will soften them slightly, but leave the bases crunchy. The toppings here range from the humble *riganada* with cherry tomatoes and feta, to the more elaborate sea urchin roe, which has sadly been almost completely fished out in the Ionian islands, but is readily available in other parts of the world. Traditionally, sea urchin bruschette are served with just the roe and olive oil, but I've added beautiful crispy sage leaves coated in butter, found in abundance on the islands.

ITHACAN SEA URCHIN AND MONASTERY BREAD BRUSCHETTE

Prep Time 5 minutes
Cooking Time 5 minutes

100 g (3½ oz) salted butter
24 sage leaves
½ small monastery sourdough baguette (or any quality
    artisan sourdough baguette)
6 tablespoons extra virgin olive oil
12 pieces (100 g/3½ oz) fresh sea urchin roe
Sea salt

—*Serves 6*

Heat the butter in a saucepan and cook the sage leaves over medium–high heat until golden brown and crispy. Remove the sage leaves and place on paper towels.

Slice the bread into twelve 8 mm (⅜ inch) thick pieces. Lightly toast the bread on both sides and place on a serving platter. Drizzle with half the olive oil, then place the sea urchin roe on top. Place two crispy sage leaves on each piece, drizzle with the remaining olive oil and garnish with salt.

Serve immediately.

RIGANADA

Prep Time 10 minutes

½ small monastery sourdough baguette (or any quality
    artisan sourdough baguette)
6 tablespoons extra virgin olive oil
160 g (5½ oz) sheep's milk feta, sliced
400 g (scant 3 cups) ripe cherry tomatoes,
    chopped into quarters
¼ red onion, sliced
2 tablespoons dried Greek oregano
Sea salt and freshly ground black pepper

—*Serves 6*

Slice the bread into twelve 8 mm (⅜ inch) thick pieces. Lightly toast the bread on both sides and place on a serving platter. Drizzle with a little olive and then top each piece with feta, cherry tomatoes and red onion. Season with sea salt and pepper.

Drizzle with a little more olive oil, sprinkle generously with oregano and drizzle more oil over the top to finish.

HARRY'S VEAL AND FETA BRUSCHETTE

Prep Time 10 minutes
Cooking Time 50 minutes

150 ml (generous ½ cup) extra virgin olive oil
1 onion, finely sliced
80 g (½ cup) finely diced carrot
70 g (½ cup) finely diced celery
2 garlic cloves, finely chopped
500 g (1 lb 2 oz) minced veal (30% fat)
250 ml (1 cup) white wine
250 ml (1 cup) Chicken stock (page 236)
3 large sprigs wild island thyme, plus a little extra
    to garnish (or cultivated thyme)
2 bay leaves
½ small monastery sourdough baguette (or any quality
    artisan sourdough baguette)
120 g (4 oz) Greek feta cheese, crumbled
Sea salt and freshly ground black pepper

—Serves 6

Place a saucepan over high heat, add half the olive oil and heat for 2 minutes. Add the onion, carrot, celery and garlic and cook over low heat until the onion is translucent.

Remove the vegetables from the pan. Add the remaining olive oil to the pan, then add the minced veal and brown the meat on all sides.

Return the vegetables to the pan. Add the white wine and cook over high heat for 2 minutes.

Add the stock, thyme and bay leaves and cook over low heat for 30 minutes. Season with salt and pepper.

Slice the bread into twelve 8 mm (⅜ inch) thick pieces. Lightly toast the bread on both sides and place on a serving platter. Top with the veal, then crumble feta cheese and extra thyme over the top.

CEPHALONIAN RAZOR CLAMS IN GENTILINI ROBOLA

Prep Time 5 minutes, plus 4 hours for soaking the clams
Cooking Time 5 minutes

1 kg (2 lb 4 oz) razor clams
125 ml (½ cup) Gentilini extra
    virgin olive oil (or any quality
    early-harvest extra virgin
    olive oil), plus extra to serve
4 garlic cloves, finely sliced
250 ml (1 cup) Gentilini Robola
    white wine (or any
    aromatic Riesling)
300 g (2 cups) cherry
    tomatoes, cut in half
3 tablespoons chopped parsley
Sea salt and freshly ground
    black pepper

Razor clams would have to be one of my favourite ingredients; I eat them as often as I can when I'm in Europe. Cephalonians feel the same, and in this dish the razor clams are married with Robola wine and olive oil – both from the acclaimed producer Gentilini – showcasing the very best that the island has to offer. If you have trouble sourcing razor clams, this dish is also beautiful with other types of clams or mussels.

To clean the razor clams, place in a large bowl and cover with cold water. Leave for a couple of hours, drain and then repeat the process.

To cook the clams, heat the oil and garlic in a large frying pan over medium heat for 1 minute, stirring continuously to ensure the garlic does not brown. Add the razor clams and stir through.

Add the white wine, and then the cherry tomatoes, crushing them with your hands as you place them in the pan. Cover with a lid, turn the heat to high and cook for 2–3 minutes, until the clams have opened.

Add the parsley, season with salt and pepper and stir gently.

Serve the clams in a bowl with their cooking juices. Drizzle with extra virgin olive oil to taste.

—Serves 4

GRILLED OCTOPUS AND BLACK-EYED BEAN SALAD
with MESSOLONGHI BOTTARGA

Prep Time 15 minutes, plus overnight soaking of beans
Cooking Time 1 hour 40 minutes

Black-eyed bean salad
280 g (1½ cups) black-eyed beans
1 bay leaf
1½ tomatoes, diced
½ red onion, finely diced
1 garlic clove, sliced
3 tablespoons chopped oregano
185 ml (¾ cup) extra virgin
    olive oil, plus extra for drizzling
3 tablespoons lemon juice
Sea salt and freshly ground
    black pepper

Grilled octopus
1 kg (2 lb 4 oz) octopus
    tentacles (large)
125 ml (½ cup) extra virgin
    olive oil

5 g (⅛ oz) Messolonghi
    bottarga, finely grated

Black-eyed beans and octopus are classic ingredients of the Greek islands, found in one version or another on almost every taverna menu. Here we've added a special element: Messolonghi bottarga, known as the Greek caviar. This is grated over the top just before serving to add a beautiful, textural burst of freshness, colour and flavour.

To make the black-eyed bean salad, place the beans and bay leaf in a pan and cover with water to 3 cm (1¼ inches) above the beans. Bring to the boil, then allow to cool and leave to soak in the refrigerator for 24 hours.

Drain the beans and rinse. Return to the clean pan and cover with water. Bring to the boil, then simmer for 40–50 minutes until tender. Drain, then cool.

Meanwhile, to make the grilled octopus, place the octopus in a large pan of boiling salted water, reduce the heat and simmer for 90 minutes until tender. Leave to cool in the cooking liquid.

Mix the cooled beans with the tomato, red onion, garlic, oregano, olive oil and lemon juice and season with salt and pepper. Toss together.

Remove the cooled octopus from the water, toss with the olive oil and season with salt and pepper. Place the octopus on a preheated grill or griddle over high heat and cook for 2–3 minutes on each side.

Serve the octopus with the black-eyed bean salad. Finish with finely grated bottarga over the top and a drizzle of extra virgin olive oil.

—Serves 6

LEFKADA SALAMI AND GRAVIERA CHEESE *with* PICKLES

Prep Time 25 minutes, plus 48 hours pickling
Cooking Time 5 minutes

400 g (14 oz) Lefkada salami, finely sliced (or any quality cured pork sausage with a high black pepper content)
240 g (8½ oz) Graviera cheese, sliced into long triangular wedges
8 slices crusty bread

Pickled baby bell peppers and long chillies
300 g (10½ oz) baby bell peppers
300 g (10½ oz) long chillies
625 ml (2½ cups) white wine vinegar
3 tablespoons caster sugar
3 tablespoons salt
2 bay leaves
1 tablespoon fennel seeds
3 garlic cloves, sliced
2 tablespoons black peppercorns

Tomato, red onion, pepper and wild caper salad
150 g (1 cup) cherry tomatoes, cut in half
¼ red onion, finely diced
40 g (¼ cup) finely diced red capsicum (pepper)
40 g (¼ cup) finely diced yellow capsicum (pepper)
40 g (¼ cup) finely diced green capsicum (pepper)
1 tablespoon wild capers
125 ml (½ cup) extra virgin olive oil
Sea salt and freshly ground black pepper

As mentioned in the chapter introduction, the Greek island of Lefkada was settled by people from the Venetian island of Burano. Despite being most well known for fishing, the people of Burano brought with them and shared their expertise in charcuterie making. Today Lefkada is renowned throughout the whole of Greece for its amazing, high-quality spicy salami, made with garlic and peppercorns.

To make the pickled baby bell peppers and long chillies, remove the cores from the peppers and shake out any seeds before packing into sterilised pickling jars. Place the long chillies in a separate pickling jar.

Put the vinegar, sugar, salt, bay leaves, fennel seeds, garlic and peppercorns in a pan with 625 ml (2½ cups) water. Bring to the boil.

Pour the hot pickling liquid over both the peppers and chillies in the jars, making sure they are completely covered. When cool, seal the jars and refrigerate for at least 48 hours.

To make the salad, combine the tomatoes, onion, capsicums and wild capers in a bowl and dress with the olive oil. Season with salt and pepper and toss together.

Serve the salami and cheese on a platter with 8 pickled bell peppers, 4 long chillies, a bowl of tomato and red onion salad and the crusty bread.

—*Serves 8*

Pasta, rice and pies

CEPHALONIAN SALT COD PIE

Prep Time 30 minutes, plus 48 hours soaking the salt cod and 40 minutes resting the dough
Cooking Time 1 hour 15 minutes

600 g (1 lb 5 oz) *baccala* (salt cod)
175 ml (¾ cup) extra virgin olive oil
3 onions, finely sliced
6 garlic cloves, chopped
2 tomatoes, peeled and chopped
250 g (1 cup) tomato paste
(concentrated purée)
100 g (½ cup) rice
3 tablespoons chopped oregano
3 tablespoons chopped parsley
100 g (2 cups) spinach, chopped
½ teaspoon allspice
Sea salt and freshly ground
black pepper

Shortcrust pastry crust
500 g (3⅓ cups) plain flour
380 g (13½ oz) butter, chilled
and diced
2 pinches salt
2 egg yolks
4 tablespoons chilled water
1 egg, lightly beaten, for egg wash

Another example of the strong Venetian influence on the cuisine of the Greek islands, the star of this recipe is, of course, the salt cod – a real legacy of the Venetian Republic and an ingredient that has been embraced in many different forms throughout the Mediterranean. Also key to this dish is the onions, which imbue a lovely sweetness that balances the saltiness of the fish.

Wash the excess salt from the cod, then soak in cold water in the fridge for 48 hours, changing the water twice daily. This process will remove most of the fish's saltiness.

Bring 800 ml (3¼ cups) water to the boil in a saucepan and poach the cod for 5–10 minutes, making sure it is covered with the water. Drain, keeping the poaching liquid. Remove all the bones from the cod and finely chop the flesh.

To make the shortcrust pastry, place the flour, butter and salt in a food processor and mix to fine crumbs. Add the egg yolks and water and process until a dough ball starts to form, taking care not to overwork the dough.

Place the dough on a lightly floured tray, cover with plastic wrap and leave to rest in the fridge for 40 minutes.

Preheat the oven to 180°C (350°F).

Pour the olive oil into a large pan and place over medium heat for 1 minute. Add the onion and cook until translucent. Add the garlic and cook for 2 minutes.

Add the cod, tomatoes and tomato paste to the pan and stir through. Add the rice and 500 ml (2 cups) of the poaching liquid. Bring to the boil and cook for another 10 minutes. Add the oregano, parsley, spinach and allspice. Cook for a further 5 minutes, then season with salt and pepper and leave to cool.

Remove the pastry from the fridge and place on a lightly floured work surface. Divide the dough in half. Using a rolling pin, roll into two 1 cm (½ inch) thick, 18 × 12 cm (7 × 4½ inch) rectangles.

Lightly grease an 18 × 12 cm (7 × 4½ inch) pie dish with olive oil. Line the dish with one piece of pastry. Pour the filling into the dish and cover with the remaining pastry rectangle. Crimp the pastry together around the edge, removing any excess. Make two small holes in the top to allow steam to escape during cooking.

Lightly whisk the egg with a dash of water and brush over the pie. Bake in the oven for 45 minutes or until the pastry is golden. Cool for 15 minutes before cutting.

—*Serves 6*

GOGGES PASTA *with* BURNT BUTTER *and* MYZITHRA SALTED RICOTTA

Prep Time 30 minutes, plus resting the dough
Cooking Time 25 minutes

Sauce
60 g (½ cup) walnuts, chopped
1 tablespoon butter
3 tablespoons olive oil
3 tablespoons dried Myzithra
   or salted goat's milk ricotta,
   grated, plus extra to garnish
Sea salt

Gogges pasta
500 g (2¾ cups) fine semolina
1 teaspoon salt
2 tablespoons olive oil

With burnt butter and salted ricotta, this dish looks and feels like it could easily belong in Italy. Having said that, two key elements are classically Greek. The first is the gogges pasta, which hails from the Peloponnese and is worth the effort to make, and the second is Myzithra – a traditional unpasteurised Greek ricotta cheese that's available both fresh (creamy and spreadable in consistency) and dried (salty and most commonly used grated over pasta, as in this dish).

Preheat the oven to 170°C (325°F). Arrange the walnuts evenly on a baking tray and cook for 3–5 minutes, or until golden brown. Take the tray out of the oven and remove the nuts from the tray to prevent over-colouring. Allow to cool completely before chopping roughly.

To make the pasta, mix together the semolina and salt in a bowl. Gradually add 250 ml (1 cup) water and knead to a smooth dough.

Add the olive oil and knead again to combine. Cover with plastic wrap and leave to rest for 30 minutes.

Divide the dough into 150 g (5½ oz) pieces; roll each piece into a log about 1.5 cm (½ inch) wide and cut into 2 cm (¾ inch) lengths.

Take a piece of dough and, using your thumb, press onto a floured wooden ridged pasta board and roll down to form a sea shell shape. If you don't have a ridged board, use a floured work surface: the pasta will be smooth but will still work. Continue until all the dough is used. Store on a floured tray, making sure the pasta shapes are not touching, until ready to cook.

Bring a large pan of salted water to the boil and cook the pasta for 12–15 minutes: the pasta is intended to be quite firm, but if you prefer a softer texture, cook for a little longer. Drain the pasta and place in a serving bowl.

Heat the butter and olive oil in a frying pan over medium heat until the butter begins to foam. Add the cheese and cook until golden brown. Pour the sauce over the pasta and sprinkle with the walnuts. Season and serve with extra cheese over the top.

—Serves 4

CORFIOT PASTITSADA *with* BUCATINI

Prep Time 10 minutes
Cooking Time 1 hour 30 minutes

125 ml (½ cup) extra virgin olive oil
4 chicken leg quarters
1 onion, finely diced
4 garlic cloves, crushed
1 cinnamon quill
¼ teaspoon ground nutmeg
1 bay leaf
100 ml (scant ½ cup) red
   wine vinegar
8 tomatoes, cored and chopped
1 tablespoon tomato paste
   (concentrated purée)
500 ml (2 cups) Chicken stock
   (page 236)
300 g (10½ oz) dried bucatini
   pasta
Grated Kefalotyri, Kefalograviera
   or Graviera cheese, to taste
Sea salt and freshly ground
   black pepper

Yet another interpretation of *pastissada* – many iterations of which are scattered throughout the Mediterranean. This one is traditionally made with cockerel, or young rooster, and is typical of what you see on almost every Greek island. Here, I'm using the whole chicken hindquarter and serving it with pasta, something not seen with *pastissada* dishes along the Croatian coast or in Italy.

Heat the olive oil in a saucepan over high heat for 1 minute. Add the chicken, skin-side-down, and cook until the skin is golden brown. Turn the chicken pieces and cook for another minute. Remove from the pan and set aside.

Turn the heat to low, add the onion and garlic and cook until the onion is translucent. Add the spices and bay leaf and cook gently for 3–4 minutes, stirring regularly.

Return the chicken to the pan and pour in the vinegar to deglaze the bottom of the pan. Stir in the tomatoes, tomato paste and stock. Season with sea salt and pepper. Cook for 40–60 minutes until the chicken is tender and starting to fall off the bone. Adjust the seasoning if required.

Cook the bucatini in a deep pan of boiling salted water until al dente.

Remove the chicken from the sauce and fold the pasta through the sauce. Serve the chicken on top of the bucatini. Sprinkle with grated Kefalotyri, Kefalograviera or Graviera cheese, to taste.

—*Serves 4*

SEAFOOD ASSYRTIKO GIOUVETSI

Prep Time 20 minutes
Cooking Time 30 minutes

125 ml (½ cup) extra virgin olive
  oil, plus extra for drizzling
310 g (2 cups) finely diced onion
60 g (1 cup) finely diced fennel
60 g (1 cup) mild red chillies, diced
1 tablespoon sweet paprika
4 garlic cloves, crushed
250 g (1½ cups) orzo pasta
375 ml (1½ cups) Assyrtiko
  white wine (or any aromatic
  white wine)
1 litre (4 cups) Crustacean
  broth (page 239)
1 tablespoon tomato paste
  (concentrated purée)
200 g (7 oz) clams
200 g (7 oz) black mussels
200 g (7 oz) calamari, cleaned
  and cut into 1 cm (½ inch)
  thick slices
200 g (7 oz) scorpion fish
  fillet (or any white fish)
200 g (7 oz) prawns, peeled,
  deveined and cut into
  2 cm (¾ inch) pieces
30 g (½ cup) chopped parsley
Sea salt and freshly ground
  black pepper

With such an abundance of quality fresh seafood, this dish is a staple on the island of Santorini. Giouvetsi is common throughout much of Greece, often with meat instead of seafood, but fish is more commonly used on many of the islands. The juggernaut indigenous Santorini white wine used in this recipe, Assyrtiko, is also a feature, and is a stunning wine to enjoy with the dish.

Heat the olive oil in a saucepan over low heat. Add the onion, fennel, chillies, paprika and garlic and cook for 3–4 minutes or until the onion is translucent. Season with salt and pepper.

Add the orzo pasta to the pan and stir through. Add the wine and stir to deglaze the pan, then cook for 4 minutes to cook off the alcohol. Add the crustacean broth and tomato paste and simmer over medium heat for 12 minutes.

Add the clams and mussels to the pan and cook for 2 minutes, then add the calamari, scorpion fish and prawns and cook for 3 minutes or until just cooked.

Adjust the seasoning if required and stir in the parsley. Drizzle with a little extra virgin olive oil to serve.

—Serves 4

IONIAN WILD WEED AND NATIVE ASPARAGUS MACARONI CHEESE

Prep Time 15 minutes
Cooking Time 1 hour 30 minutes

125 g (4½ oz) dried pennette pasta
150 ml (generous ½ cup)
    extra virgin olive oil
200 g (7 oz) wild weeds
    – any combination of Greek
    horta greens, Greek *vlita*
    (amaranth), spinach, beetroot
    leaves, kale, any chard or silver
    beet, roughly chopped
200 g (7 oz) native asparagus,
    roughly chopped (or regular
    green asparagus)
1 large leek, chopped
2 garlic cloves, finely chopped
225 g (8 oz) Greek feta
    cheese, crumbled
225 g (8 oz) Graviera or
    Kefalograviera cheese,
    finely grated
225 g (8 oz) fresh ricotta cheese
Pinch of nutmeg
4 filo pastry sheets
40 g (1½ oz) butter, melted
25 g (scant ¼ cup) sesame seeds
Sea salt and freshly ground
    black pepper

Pastitsio is a classic baked pasta dish in Greece, usually comprising pennette or macaroni, minced meat and béchamel sauce. This is a fantastic vegetarian version, which also draws on key elements from another Greek favourite – wild weed pie. I've omitted *pastitsio's* béchamel and replaced the meat with a range of bright and wonderful wild greens, including the indigenous *horta*, *vlita* and native asparagus. Feel free to use as many greens as you like, with chard, spinach and green asparagus making great substitutes.

Preheat the oven to 180°C (350°F).

Bring a large pot of salted water to the boil and cook the pennette pasta until just tender. Drain, toss in 3 tablespoons of the olive oil and set aside.

Wash the wild weed vegetables and asparagus in cold water.

Heat the remaining olive oil in a large frying pan over low heat, add the leek and garlic and cook for 5–10 minutes until the leek has completely softened. Add the wild weeds and asparagus and cook until the leafy greens have wilted and the asparagus softened. Season with sea salt and pepper and cook, stirring constantly, over low heat for another 5 minutes. (Be careful with the seasoning as the cheeses added later will add salt.)

Transfer the mixture to a bowl and add the feta, Graviera or Kefalograviera cheese, ricotta and nutmeg and stir well. Mix in the cooked pennette. Adjust the seasoning if required and spoon into a lightly greased 24 × 32 cm (9½ x 12½ inch) baking dish.

Brush each sheet of filo on both sides with melted butter. Lay the filo sheets on top of the wild weed and asparagus mixture and sprinkle with sesame seeds.

Bake for 55 minutes, or until golden.

—*Serves 6*

SPICY LOBSTER LINGUINI

Prep Time 25 minutes
Cooking Time 1 hour

1–1.2 kg (2 lb 4 oz–2 lb 10 oz)
  live lobster
150 ml (generous ½ cup)
  extra virgin olive oil
1 white onion, finely diced
4 garlic cloves, chopped
125 ml (½ cup) Metaxa brandy
  (or any quality brandy)
250 ml (1 cup) white wine
6 ripe tomatoes, diced
500 ml (2 cups) Crustacean
  broth (page 239)
½ teaspoon dried chilli flakes
  (or to taste)
25 g (½ cup) basil leaves, chopped
2 tablespoons chopped parsley
600 g (1 lb 5 oz) dried linguini
1 tablespoon butter
Sea salt and freshly ground
  black pepper

This is a special occasion dish, usually served in high-end restaurants and showcasing some of the best flavours of Mediterranean Greece, including fresh lobster and Metaxa, an iconic Greek brandy. I've taken the liberty of adding a dash of chilli flakes – something not commonly found in Greek cuisine – adding a lovely heat to the dish.

Place the lobster into the freezer for 10 minutes before cooking.

Fill a large pot with salted water and bring to the boil over high heat. Place the lobster in the water and cook for approximately 5–7 minutes, depending on the size. Remove the lobster and place into iced water to stop the cooking process.

When the lobster is chilled, cut in half and carefully remove the meat from the tail. The meat will be largely raw except for the flesh near the shell. Dice into 2.5 cm (1 inch) pieces, keeping the head for serving.

To make the sauce, heat the olive oil in a saucepan over low heat, add the onion and cook until translucent. Add the garlic and cook for 1 minute. Add the brandy and cook for 2 minutes. Add the white wine and cook for 2 minutes. Add the tomatoes, broth, chilli flakes, basil and parsley and simmer over medium heat for 25–30 minutes.

Before serving, cook the lobster head in a hot oven, in boiling water, or under a hot grill for 10 minutes.

Meanwhile, cook the pasta in a large pan of boiling salted water for 9–13 minutes or until al dente. Just before the pasta will be ready, add the lobster meat and butter to the sauce, giving the lobster 3 minutes to cook through before serving. Season with salt and pepper.

Drain the pasta and toss through the sauce. Serve on a platter and decorate with the warmed lobster head.

—*Serves 4*

Mains

CYPRIAN SLOW-COOKED CALAMARI STIFADO

Prep Time 10 minutes
Cooking Time 1 hour 10 minutes

250 ml (1 cup) extra virgin olive
    oil, plus extra for drizzling
1 onion, finely diced
4 garlic cloves, crushed
250 ml (1 cup) Xynisteri white wine
    (or any quality dry white wine)
1.6 kg (8 cups) chopped tomatoes
2 tablespoons tomato paste
    (concentrated purée)
2 bay leaves
½ tablespoon Greek oregano
1 kg (2 lb 4 oz) small whole
    calamari, cleaned
8 baby potatoes, cut in half
2 tablespoons chopped
    parsley (optional)
Sea salt and freshly ground
    black pepper

The method of slow cooking in Greece is known as *stifado*; in Italy it's *stufato*, based on the Italian word for stove – *'stufa'*. While commonly reserved for meats, slow cooking can be used for calamari and octopus too, delivering stunning results. The base ingredients of white wine, olive oil, bay leaf, onion, garlic and tomato create great flavour in this dish. For a more intense version, the white wine can be substituted for any quality medium-bodied red wine – my wife's favourite!

Place the olive oil and onion in a large saucepan over low heat and cook until the onion is translucent.

Add the garlic and cook for 1 minute. Add the white wine and cook for 2 minutes. Add the tomatoes, tomato paste, bay leaves, oregano and 500 ml (2 cups) water and bring to a simmer.

Add the calamari and potatoes and cook over low heat for 30–60 minutes, or until tender. Season with salt and pepper and, if you like, garnish with chopped parsley. Finish with a drizzle of extra virgin olive oil.

—*Serves 4*

ITHACAN SLOW-ROASTED ISLAND GOAT *with* FRESH OREGANO

Prep Time 15 minutes
Cooking Time 5 hours 10 minutes

1.4 kg (3 lb 2 oz) kid goat shoulder, bone in and shankless
8 garlic cloves, 2 finely chopped, 6 left whole
25 g (1 cup) fresh island oregano (or any fresh oregano)
250 ml (1 cup) lemon juice
250 ml (1 cup) extra virgin olive oil, plus extra for drizzling
500 ml (2 cups) Chicken stock (page 236)
1 kg (2 lb 4 oz) potatoes, peeled and sliced 2 cm (¾ inch) thick
Sea salt and freshly ground black pepper

Goat from Ithaca, the island where my wife Krissoula's family still lives, would have to be some of the very best meat I've ever eaten. Krissoula's cousins are shepherds, and their herd of goats eat any number of the roughly 33 different wild herbs on the island, including thyme and sage, which imparts a very distinctive and unique flavour into the meat. Every time we visit we feast on a goat, spit roasted until the meat is literally falling off the bone. It's absolute heaven, and always a highlight of our trip. If you're not lucky enough to have a spit roast at your disposal, oven roasting will create a stunning result too.

Preheat the oven to 200°C (400°F).

Smother the goat shoulder with the chopped garlic and season with salt and black pepper.

Form a bed in a roasting tin with half the oregano and the whole garlic cloves. Place the goat shoulder on top. Drizzle with lemon juice and half the olive oil.

Cover the tin with foil and roast for 30 minutes. Reduce the oven to 150°C (300°F) and add the stock to the roasting tin. Continue to cook, covered, for a further 3½–4 hours, turning halfway, until the goat is very tender. Remove the foil and increase the oven temperature to 180°C (350°F) for the last 20 minutes to colour the meat.

Remove the goat from the tin, cover with foil and keep warm.

Place the potatoes in the same roasting tin and drizzle with the remaining oil. Season with salt and pepper and return to the oven at 180°C (350°F). Roast for 40 minutes, turning halfway through the cooking.

Serve the goat with the roasted potatoes and pan juices, garnished with the remaining chopped oregano and extra olive oil, if you like.

—*Serves 8*

SWEET-AND-SOUR RED MULLET FROM CRETE

Prep Time 5 minutes
Cooking Time 25 minutes

4 large red mullets, scaled
   and gutted
½ tablespoon sea salt
150 g (1 cup) plain flour
125 ml (½ cup) extra virgin olive oil
4 garlic cloves, sliced
2 sprigs rosemary
125 ml (½ cup) white wine vinegar
150 g (scant 1 cup) black raisins

This is a dish you'll find throughout most of the formerly Venetian-ruled Greek islands, not to mention the Republic's other key Mediterranean territories. The original Venetian dish *'in saor'*, which means 'to add flavour' (called *savoro* in Greece), was really borne out of necessity, with fishermen using vinegar in an attempt to preserve the abundance of freshly caught fish. In Italy and Greece less vinegar is used today than in the past and, unlike the Venetian version, Greeks do not often incorporate onions, but add their own unique touch with rosemary and garlic instead.

Preheat the oven to 180°C (350°F).

Season the red mullet with sea salt, then coat with a dusting of flour.

Heat half the olive oil in a large frying pan for 1 minute. Add the fish and cook on each side for 2 minutes.

Transfer the fish to a baking tray and roast until just cooked – the timing will depend on the size of the fish: a medium fish will take 5 minutes to cook, a larger fish will take 10 minutes. The meat at the back of the fish head should just be coming away from the bone.

Meanwhile, heat the remaining olive oil, garlic and rosemary in a small pan over low heat for 1 minute. Add the vinegar and raisins and then simmer for 10 minutes.

Place the fish on a serving dish and pour the vinegar dressing over the top. Let it cool and serve the fish at room temperature.

—Serves 4

CORFU-STYLE JOHN DORY
COOKED IN WHITE WINE *with* WILD GREENS

Prep Time 10 minutes
Cooking Time 50 minutes

300 ml (1¼ cups) extra virgin
    olive oil
½ white onion, thinly sliced
8 garlic cloves, chopped
1 cup (250 ml) Corfiot Kakotrygis
    white wine (or any quality dry
    white wine)
125 ml (½ cup) lemon juice
500 g (1 lb 2 oz) potatoes, peeled
    and sliced into 2 cm (¾ inch)
    thick pieces
500 ml (2 cups) Fish stock
    (page 236)
1 tablespoon picked oregano
1 tablespoon picked rosemary
600 g (1 lb 5 oz) John Dory fillets
Sea salt and freshly ground
    black pepper

Wild greens
900 g (2 lb) Greek *vlita* (amaranth)
3 tablespoons extra virgin olive oil
Juice of 1 lemon
2 teaspoons sea salt

This is a classic example of *'in bianco'*, a term used in Italian cooking to denote a 'white' dish – that is, where tomatoes or red wine aren't used. It usually suggests the inclusion of white wine and has, over generations, been wholeheartedly embraced in Corfu, by far the most Venetian influenced of all the Greek islands. This recipe uses fillets, but it's also fantastic with a whole fish – you'll just need to adjust the cooking time accordingly.

Heat half the olive oil in a large frying pan over low heat. Add the onion and half the garlic and cook until soft and translucent. Add the wine and half the lemon juice and cook until the wine has almost evaporated.

Stir in the potatoes and cook for 2 minutes. Add the fish stock, half the oregano and half the rosemary and season with salt and pepper. Turn the heat to medium and cook for 15 minutes or until the potatoes are cooked through.

Meanwhile, for the wild greens, trim the thick stems from the base of the amaranth and rinse well. Bring a large pot of salted water to the boil. Add the greens and cook for 10–15 minutes until tender. Drain and dress with the olive oil, lemon juice and salt. Serve warm or at room temperature.

Place the John Dory on top of the potatoes in the pan. Add the remaining garlic and drizzle with the remaining oil. Cook for about 5 minutes, until the fish is just cooked through.

Mix the remaining lemon juice with a little extra virgin olive oil and toss with the remaining oregano and rosemary.

Serve the John Dory with the potatoes and pan juices on a platter. Garnish with the fresh herbs and lemon juice mixture and serve alongside the wild greens.

—Serves 4

RABBIT STIFADO *with* GRAVIERA CHEESE *and* POLENTA BREAD

Prep Time 40 minutes, plus 2–3 hours marinating
Cooking Time 3 hours 20 minutes

1–1.5 kg (2 lb 4 oz–3 lb 5 oz) whole rabbit, cut into 8 pieces
150 ml (generous ½ cup) white wine vinegar
160 g (5½ oz) butter
155 g (1 cup) diced onion
4 garlic cloves, finely diced
155 g (1 cup) diced carrot
140 g (1 cup) diced celery
135 g (1 cup) diced leek
500 ml (2 cups) red wine
3 bay leaves
2 cloves
1 cinnamon quill
3 tablespoons tomato paste (concentrated purée)
1.5 litres (6 cups) Chicken stock (page 236)
250 g (9 oz) Graviera cheese, broken into 2 cm (¾ inch) pieces
Sea salt and freshly ground black pepper

Polenta bread
150 g (1 cup) plain flour
380 g (2 cups) polenta (fine grain)
2½ teaspoons baking powder
1 teaspoon salt
1½ tablespoons honey
3 eggs
600 ml (2½ cups) Buttermilk (page 243)
300 g (10½ oz) butter, melted
180 g (6½ oz) quality feta, crumbled

Rabbit is a very popular ingredient for Greek *stifado*, which is made in many regions. In this recipe the rabbit is served with polenta bread, traditionally eaten in Greece as a dessert. I've tweaked it to create a more modern, savoury version, which is fantastic with most slow-cooked braised dishes.

Place the rabbit in a large bowl, cover with the vinegar and marinate for 2–3 hours. Drain and pat dry with paper towels.

Heat a large flameproof casserole dish over medium heat. Add the butter and rabbit pieces and cook gently for 5 minutes, turning as the rabbit browns. Lightly season with salt and pepper (not too much salt as the Graviera cheese is salty).

Remove the rabbit from the dish. Add the onion, garlic, carrot, celery and leek to the dish and cook until starting to brown. Return the rabbit to the dish and then add the wine, bay leaves, cloves, cinnamon and tomato paste and cook for about 10 minutes until the wine has almost evaporated.

Add the stock and cook over low heat for 3 hours or until the meat is falling off the bone.

Add the Graviera cheese and cook for 10 minutes until the cheese is soft but not completely melted.

Meanwhile, preheat the oven to 180°C (350°F).

For the polenta bread, mix together the flour, polenta, baking powder and salt in a large mixing bowl.

Whisk together the honey, eggs, buttermilk and 4 tablespoons of the melted butter in a bowl.

Heat a 24 × 12 × 6 cm (10 × 5 × 2 inch) baking dish in the oven. When hot, coat the inside of the baking dish thoroughly with the remaining butter (I use paper towels to get into all corners of the dish).

Combine the honey mixture with the polenta mixture and 100 g (3½ oz) of the feta cheese, then pour into the baking dish, spreading evenly. Sprinkle the remaining feta over the top and bake for 25–35 minutes, until cooked through.

Arrange the rabbit on a serving platter and serve with the cooking juices and polenta bread.

Note
Leftover polenta bread is great toasted and served with fresh butter.

—Serves 6

ROASTED PORK LOIN *with* SLOW-BRAISED ARTICHOKES *and* BABY BROAD BEANS

Prep Time 20 minutes, plus overnight refrigeration of pork
Cooking Time 1 hour 30 minutes

3 kg (6 lb 12 oz) rolled pork loin (ask a butcher to roll and tie a pork loin with the belly attached in 3–4 cm (1¼–1½ inch) intervals and score the skin between the ties)
3 tablespoons sea salt
100 ml (scant ½ cup) extra virgin olive oil

Slow-braised artichokes and baby broad beans
1 lemon, cut in half
3 globe artichokes
500 g (1 lb 2 oz) baby broad beans
350 ml (scant 1½ cups) extra virgin olive oil, plus extra for drizzling
2 onions, roughly chopped
4 garlic cloves, finely chopped
3 ripe tomatoes, cored and roughly chopped
Sea salt and freshly ground black pepper

I'm sorry to say that not many people cook for me these days. Many other chefs will tell you they have the same problem. Thankfully, my mother-in-law, Maria, is an exception, and a wonderful one at that. This is probably my favourite dish of hers, although she has many greats. I particularly love the slow-braised artichokes and broad beans – a simple but fantastic combination – and if it wasn't for Maria, I wouldn't know the joy of cooking and eating broad beans whole. To cook them this way, choose small, early-harvest broad beans as they will be the most tender.

Preheat the oven to 250°C (500°F).

For the roasted pork loin, bring 5 litres (170 fl oz) water to the boil. Place the pork on a cooling rack over a sink and carefully pour the boiling water over the pork skin, turning to ensure it is all rendered. Rub the sea salt into the skin and refrigerate, uncovered, overnight.

Remove from the refrigerator and bring the pork to room temperature. Add the olive oil to a roasting tin and heat in the oven for 8 minutes. Remove from the oven and place the pork in the tin, turning as the skin blisters all over. Reduce the oven to 200°C (400°F) and roast the pork for 90 minutes, turning every 10–15 minutes. Let the pork rest for 30–40 minutes before carving.

Meanwhile, for the braised artichokes and broad beans, squeeze half the lemon into a bowl of cold water. Remove the outer leaves of the artichokes, then, using a spoon, scoop out the centre choke and peel the stem with a vegetable peeler. Rub the artichokes all over with the lemon half as you do this to prevent them discolouring. Cut the artichokes into quarters and store in the cold lemon water.

Top and tail the young broad beans (do not shell or peel). Leave whole if they are small but cut in half, on an angle, if they are large. You want them to be no longer than a large green bean.

Place the extra virgin olive oil and onion in a large saucepan over low heat and cook until translucent. Add the garlic and cook for 1 minute. Stir in the tomato.

Drain the artichokes and add to the pan. Add the broad beans and season with salt and pepper. Add enough water to almost cover the ingredients – don't add too much water, or you'll dilute the flavour of the dish and its liquid.

Bring to a simmer and gently cook the artichokes and beans for 25 minutes or until completely tender, stirring gently throughout.

Slice the pork into 2.5 cm (1 inch) thick slices. Serve with the braised artichokes and broad beans and season with olive oil and freshly ground black pepper.

—Serves 6

Dolci

CORFU MAVRODAPHNE ZABAGLIONE
with ROSEWATER WALNUT BISCUITS

Prep Time 15 minutes
Cooking Time 25 minutes

Walnut biscuits
185 g (1½ cups) icing
  (confectioners') sugar, plus
  3 tablespoons for the biscuits
125 g (4½ oz) butter, softened
½ teaspoon rosewater
125 g (scant 1 cup) plain flour
90 g (¾ cup) walnuts, chopped

Zabaglione
8 egg yolks
110 g (½ cup) caster sugar
125 ml (½ cup) Mavrodaphne
  sweet wine (or any quality
  fortified sweet red wine)

Zabaglione, a light dessert made with egg yolks, sugar and Marsala, is famous in Italy – and in Corfu too. It is yet another linguistic and culinary marriage between the two countries. Being the most Italian of the Greek islands, I wasn't surprised to spot this dish in Corfu: as far as I've seen it's the only one of the Greek islands to offer it as part of its dessert repertoire. They do a great job of it, too, using Greece's indigenous fortified sweet wine variety, Mavrodaphne, in place of Marsala.

To make the walnut biscuits, preheat the oven to 180°C (350°F) and spread the icing sugar evenly over a tray.

Whisk together the butter and rosewater in a mixing bowl. Sift together the flour and 3 tablespoons icing sugar, then beat into the butter. Fold in the walnuts.

Roll the dough into 2.5 cm (1 inch) balls and place on a baking tray 5 cm (2 inches) apart. Bake in the oven for 12 minutes. Roll the biscuits in the icing sugar on the tray and leave to cool.

To make the zabaglione, half fill a pan with water and bring to a simmer over medium heat. Whisk the egg yolks, sugar and wine together in a large heatproof bowl. Place the bowl over the pan of simmering water and whisk for 10 minutes, until the mixture thickens to the consistency of a light custard.

Pour the zabaglione into serving glasses. When the biscuits are cool, roll again in the icing sugar and serve with the zabaglione.

—Serves 4

IONIAN PLUM CROSTATA

Prep Time 30 minutes, plus 30 minutes to rest the dough
Cooking Time 45 minutes

180 g (6½ oz) butter, softened
165 g (1⅓ cups) icing
    (confectioners') sugar
2 eggs
½ tablespoon vanilla extract
260 g (1¾ cups) 00 flour, sifted
1 pinch of salt
125 g (1¼ cups) ground almonds

Plum jam
500 g (1 lb 2 oz) plums,
    quartered, stones removed
1 tablespoon lemon juice
625 g (scant 3 cups) caster sugar

Whipped cream
250 ml (1 cup) thick
    (double) cream
1 tablespoon icing (confectioners')
    sugar, sifted
Seeds from ½ vanilla pod

Known locally as *pasta flora*, this dish is a direct relative of Italy's *pasta frolla* – meaning shortcrust pastry, the basis for tarts like this one. I've used plums in this recipe: they are beautiful and most commonly used in Cephalonia. Jams from almost any other fruit can be substituted. Use the best fruit available and in season.

Beat the butter and icing sugar together until smooth. Beat in 1 egg and the vanilla extract. Add the flour, salt and ground almonds and mix until a rough dough starts to form.

Turn the dough out onto a lightly floured work surface and knead to a dough. Place on a floured tray, cover with plastic wrap and refrigerate for 30 minutes.

Meanwhile, make the plum jam. In a heavy-based large, deep saucepan, bring the plums, 125 ml (½ cup) water and the lemon juice to the boil. Add the sugar and cook for 20 minutes.

Preheat the oven to 180°C (350°F) and grease a 26 cm (10½ inch) tart tin with a little butter.

Remove the pastry from the fridge and divide into two balls. On a lightly floured bench, use a rolling pin to roll out one ball into a 30 cm (12 inch) circle.

Line the base of the tart tin with the pastry circle and spread 640 g (2 cups) of the plum jam evenly over the base. Roll the other dough ball into a 26 cm (10½ inch) rectangle and cut into 2 cm (¾ inch) wide strips. Lay the pastry strips on top of the tart in a lattice pattern.

Beat the remaining egg and brush over the top of the tart to glaze. Bake the tart for 25 minutes until golden.

Meanwhile, to make the whipped cream, whisk the cream and sifted icing sugar until stiff. Stir in the vanilla seeds.

To serve, cut the tart into slices and serve with the whipped cream.

Note
This recipe makes more jam than is needed for the crostata. Store the extra jam in an airtight container in the refrigerator.

—Serves 8

ORANGE SPONGE CAKE *with* CANDIED GRAPES

Prep Time 15 minutes
Cooking Time 40 minutes

Sponge cake
60 g (2 oz) butter
2 tablespoons orange zest
125 g (scant 1 cup) plain flour
1 pinch salt
4 eggs
125 g (generous ½ cup)
    caster sugar

Candied grapes
250 g (9 oz) seedless grapes
250 g (generous 1 cup) sugar
10 g (¼ oz) pectin
1 teaspoon lemon juice

Whipped cream
250 ml (1 cup) thick
    (double) cream
1 tablespoon icing
    (confectioners') sugar
Seeds from ½ vanilla pod

While an Italian pastry chef in the employment of a Genoese marquis in Spain is said to have invented the first sponge cake, the rest of the Western world has certainly embraced it. Greece is no exception, with numerous variations of the sponge cake, or *pantespani* as the Greeks call it, to be found throughout the country. As in this recipe, in Greece sponge cake is usually served with some kind of syrup, and often with candied fruit, like these amazing grapes.

To make the sponge cake, first preheat the oven to 180°C (350°F).

Melt the butter and let it cool slightly. Grease a 24 cm (9½ inch) round cake tin with a little of the butter. Add the orange zest to the remaining butter.

Sift the flour and salt together into a bowl.

In a heatproof bowl, beat the eggs and sugar until pale.

Half fill a saucepan with water and bring to a simmer over low heat. Place the bowl of eggs and sugar on top of the pan, ensuring the water does not touch the bottom of the bowl. Using an electric mixer, whisk for 10 minutes – the mixture should triple in volume.

Remove the bowl from the pan and sift in half the flour. Fold in gently with a metal spoon, then repeat with the remaining flour. Add the melted butter and orange zest and fold through again.

Pour the batter into the cake tin and bake for 25 minutes.

Meanwhile, to make the candied grapes, put the grapes, sugar and 50 ml (scant ¼ cup) water in a pan and bring to a slow boil over low heat. Add the pectin and lemon juice and cook for around 10 minutes until it has a thick consistency: do not over-boil.

To make the whipped cream, whisk together the cream and sifted icing sugar until stiff peaks form. Stir in the vanilla seeds.

Remove the cake from the oven and cool on a rack. To serve, cut the cake into slices and serve with a tablespoon of candied grapes and whipped cream.

—Serves 8

CORFIOT ALMOND AND GLACÉ KUMQUAT TORRONE

Prep Time 1 hour, plus 1 hour refrigeration
Cooking Time 15 minutes

600 g (scant 4 cups) whole blanched almonds
200 g (7 oz) glacé kumquats (or glacé clementines or glacé oranges)
250 g (¾ cup) quality honey
60 g (2 oz) egg whites
Seeds from 1 vanilla pod
410 g (scant 2 cups) caster sugar
6 sheets of rice paper
200 g (7 oz) good-quality 55% dark chocolate (optional)

The word 'torrone' or 'nougat' in Greek is *'mandolato'*, and comes from the Venetian term *'torrone mandorlato'*. This recipe hails from Corfu, famous for both its kumquat cultivation and nougat production and features the amazing glacé kumquats produced on the island. Best enjoyed with an espresso, this torrone is delicious.

Preheat the oven to 180°C (350°F).

Place the almonds on a baking tray and toast in the oven until golden brown. Keep in a warm place in the kitchen.

Drain the kumquats and remove any excess syrup. Slice the kumquats into 1 cm (½ inch) slices.

Place the honey in a small saucepan over medium heat and bring to 121°C (250°F) on a sugar thermometer.

Beat the egg whites and vanilla seeds in an electric mixer until soft peaks form. Slowly pour the honey into the egg whites and beat until stiff peaks form.

Meanwhile, place 100 ml water with the sugar in a small saucepan and bring up to 147°C (297°F). Slowly pour this into the meringue base until fully incorporated, firm and glossy. Fold in the warm toasted almonds and kumquats.

Place 3 rice paper sheets, about 23 × 16 cm (9 × 6¼ inches), on the work surface. Place a third of the mixture on each sheet, about 1 cm (½ inch) high. With a damp spatula, spread the mix evenly. Cover each one with another rice paper sheet and gently press with a rolling pin. Place in the fridge for 1 hour.

Brush a sharp bread knife with oil and slice into 8 × 1 cm (3¼ x ½ inch) pieces.

Gently melt the chocolate in a double boiler or in the microwave until just melted. Place in a piping bag and drizzle over the nougat. Alternatively, dip whole pieces of the nougat into the chocolate or leave some nougat pieces without any chocolate glaze, for some variety.

Wrap the torrone in plastic wrap and store in an airtight container in the fridge for up to 3 weeks.

—MAKES 54 pieces

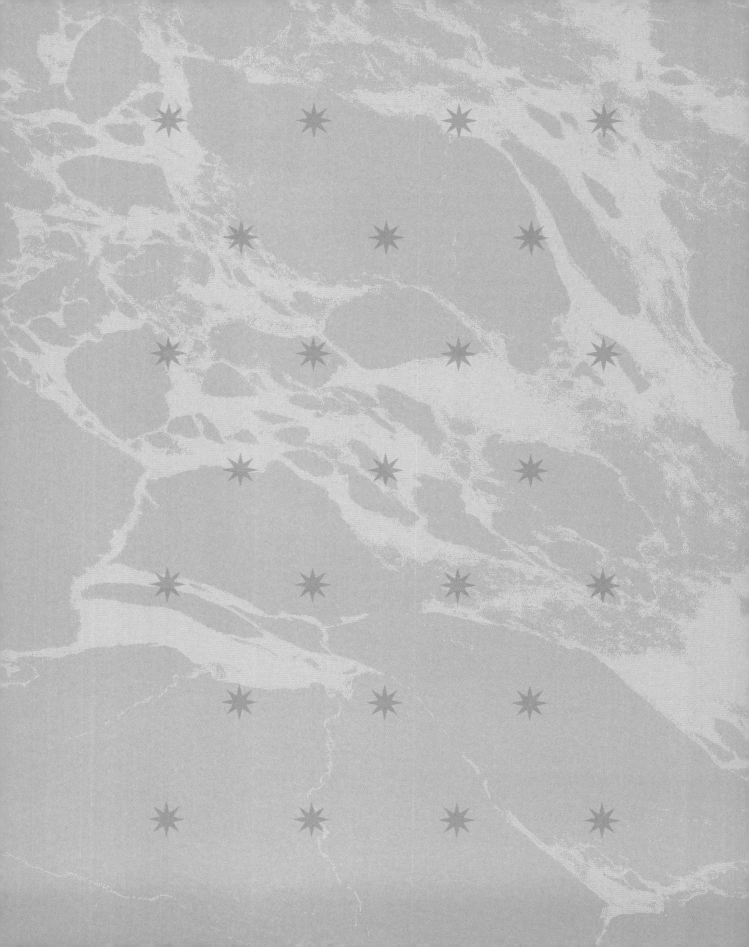

BASE
RECIPES

V

CHICKEN STOCK

Prep Time 15 minutes, plus 2–3 hours chilling
Cooking Time 2½–3 hours

1–1.2 kg (2 lb 4 oz–2 lb 10 oz)
   boiling hen
1 kg (2 lb 4 oz) fresh chicken
   bones, thoroughly washed
100 g (3½ oz) carrot,
   roughly chopped
100 g (3½ oz) celery
   stalks, roughly chopped
100 g (3½ oz) leek,
   roughly chopped
100 g (3½ oz) onion,
   roughly chopped
100 g (3½ oz) Parmigiano
   Reggiano cheese
   rind (optional)
3 Italian parsley sprigs
Sea salt, to taste

Place all the ingredients in a large saucepan with 4 litres (16 cups) water and bring to the boil. Lower the heat and simmer without a lid for 2½–3 hours. Skim away the excess fat and other particles that come to the surface during the cooking process.

Remove the chicken, shred the meat from the bones for later use (discard the skin and bones), strain the liquid through a fine strainer and refrigerate for 2–3 hours or until it has a consistency similar to set jelly. Excess fat will solidify at the top of the refrigerated stock: remove this with a spoon and discard before using the stock.

Chicken stock can be made in advance and frozen in an airtight container for up to 2 months.

Note
The shredded chicken meat can be used in soups or pie fillings.

—*MAKES approximately 2.5 litres (10 cups)*

FISH STOCK

Prep Time 20 minutes
Cooking Time 1–1½ hours

3 tablespoons olive oil
100 g (3½ oz) carrot,
   roughly chopped
100 g (3½ oz) celery
   stalks, roughly chopped
100 g (3½ oz) leek,
   roughly chopped
100 g (3½ oz) onion,
   roughly chopped
2 kg (4 lb 8 oz) fresh snapper
   bones (including heads),
   washed thoroughly and
   roughly chopped
100 ml (scant ½ cup) dry
   white wine
2 bay leaves
5 black peppercorns
3 Italian parsley sprigs
Sea salt, to taste

Heat the olive oil in a large saucepan over medium heat. Place all the vegetables in the saucepan and sauté until the leek and onion are soft and translucent. Add the fish bones and sauté for about 5 minutes, then add the wine. Cook until the wine has evaporated, then add 4 litres (16 cups) water, the bay leaves, peppercorns, parsley and sea salt. Bring to the boil. Lower the heat and slowly simmer without a lid for 40 minutes. Skim away the excess fat and other particles that come to the surface during the cooking process.

Discard the larger fish bones and strain the liquid through a fine strainer. Strain again through a fine sieve or with muslin to make sure all the bones are removed. Use the broth straight away or refrigerate.

Fish stock can be made in advance and frozen in an airtight container for up to 2 months.

—*MAKES approximately 3.5 litres (14 cups)*

VEGETABLE STOCK

Prep Time 20 minutes
Cooking Time ½–1 hour

Place all the ingredients in a large saucepan with 4 litres (16 cups) water and bring to the boil. Lower the heat and slowly simmer for 30–60 minutes. Strain through a fine sieve. Use the broth straight away or refrigerate.

Vegetable stock can be made in advance and frozen in an airtight container for up to 2 months.

—*MAKES approximately 3 litres (12 cups)*

200 g (7 oz) parsnip, roughly chopped
200 g (7 oz) turnip, roughly chopped
300 g (7 oz) carrots, roughly chopped
100 g (3½ oz) fennel bulb, roughly chopped
300 g (10½ oz) celery stalks, roughly chopped
200 g (7 oz) leek, roughly chopped
200 g (7 oz) onion, roughly chopped
1 bay leaf
2 thyme sprigs
2 Italian parsley sprigs
5 black peppercorns

BEEF OR VEAL STOCK

Prep Time 1½ hours, plus 2–3 hours chilling
Cooking Time 4½–5½ hours

Preheat the oven to 150°C (300°F).

Place the bones and trimmings in a roasting tin and bake until nicely browned (approximately 1–1½ hours). Heat the olive oil in a deep heavy-based frying pan and sauté the onion, carrot, celery and garlic until they are nicely browned.

Deglaze the roasting tin with a little water, then transfer to a large saucepan and add 4 litres (16 cups) water with all the other ingredients. Bring to the boil, then lower the heat and slowly simmer without a lid for 3–4 hours. Skim away the excess fat and other particles that come to the surface of the liquid during the cooking process. Strain the liquid through a fine strainer and refrigerate for 2–3 hours or until it has a consistency similar to set jelly. Excess fat will solidify at the top of the refrigerated stock. Remove this with a spoon and discard before using the stock.

Beef (or veal) stock can be made in advance and frozen in an airtight container for up to 2 months.

—*MAKES approximately 2.5 litres (10 cups)*

2 kg (4 lb 8 oz) fresh beef bones and trimmings (replace the beef bones with veal bones to make veal stock)
2 tablespoons olive oil
100 g (3½ oz) onion, roughly chopped
100 g (3½ oz) carrot, roughly chopped
100 g (3½ oz) celery stalks, roughly chopped
40 g (1½ oz) garlic cloves, roughly chopped
2 ripe tomatoes, roughly chopped
2 bay leaves
5 black peppercorns
2 thyme sprigs
2 Italian parsley sprigs

CRUSTACEAN BROTH

Prep Time 20 minutes
Cooking Time 1¼ hours

Preheat the oven to 180°C (350°F).

Place the prawn shells in a small roasting tin and toss with the olive oil. Roast for 10–15 minutes or until golden, stirring occasionally.

In a large saucepan, heat the oil over medium–high heat and add the vegetables and garlic. Add the prawn shells and tomato paste and sauté for 1 minute. Add the snapper bones and blue swimmer crabs and sauté for about 5 minutes before adding the dry white wine. Cook until the wine has evaporated, then add the tomatoes and 3.5 litres (14 cups) water. Bring the stock to the boil, then reduce to a slow simmer and cook for 40–60 minutes, skimming occasionally.

Discard the large fish bones and strain the liquid through a fine strainer. Make sure you press the prawn shells while straining as extra flavour is stored in them. Strain again through a fine sieve or muslin to make sure all the bones are removed. Use the broth straight away or refrigerate.

Crustacean broth can be made in advance and frozen in an airtight container for up to 2 months.

—*MAKES approximately 3 litres (12 cups)*

300 g (10½ oz) prawn shells
3 tablespoons olive oil
2½ tablespoons extra virgin olive oil
200 g (7 oz) onion, roughly chopped
150 g (5½ oz) carrot, roughly chopped
50 g (2 oz) celery stalks, roughly chopped
40 g (1½ oz) garlic cloves, roughly chopped
200 g (7 oz) tomato paste (concentrated purée)
2 kg (4 lb 8 oz) fresh snapper bones (including heads), washed thoroughly and roughly chopped
2 whole blue swimmer crabs, cleaned and cut into quarters
100 ml (scant ½ cup) dry white wine
1.2 kg (2 lb 10 oz) ripe tomatoes, roughly chopped

FRESH EGG PASTA DOUGH

Prep Time 1 hour, plus 30 minutes chilling

330 g (2¼ cups) plain flour,
    plus extra for kneading
    and rolling
70 g (⅓ cup) fine semolina
½ teaspoon fine sea salt
4 × 60 g (2 oz) free-range eggs

Combine the flour, semolina and sea salt and place on a work surface or large wooden board. The flour should form a peaked mound. With your hand, make a hole in the top of the mound so that it resembles a volcano. This hole needs to be big enough to house the eggs.

Break the eggs into the hole. With your hands or with a fork, gently beat the eggs, then add the flour. This is done by moving your hand in a circular motion, slowly incorporating the flour from the inside wall of the mound. Don't worry if it looks a mess: this is normal. Once fully combined, knead a bit more flour into the dough if it feels wet or sticky. Set the dough aside and clean the work surface.

Dust flour onto the work surface and knead the dough for another 5 minutes. Wrap in plastic wrap and refrigerate for at least 30 minutes.

To roll out the pasta, cut the rested dough into six 100 g (3½ oz) pieces. Flatten each piece with the ends of your fingers and the palm of your hand, then commence passing the dough through a pasta machine, starting with the widest setting and then slowly reducing the width. This will make the pasta sheets increasingly thinner. The pasta sheets will appear quite rough at first, but as you pass them through the machine they will becoming increasingly smooth. Pass the pasta through the machine at each setting at least twice.

After about the third setting, fold the pasta and pass it through the machine several more times as it needs to be quite smooth. Folding also helps to create a flat edge to the pasta and, as you fold and pass it through, make sure that the dough is as wide as the rollers. This is especially important when pasta sheets are to be used for baked or filled pasta. Throughout this process it is important to dust the pasta sheets with a little extra flour. If the dough feels wet, increase the amount of flour used to dust the sheets. This will make a drier dough.

For flat pasta, such as pappardelle, tagliatelle, linguini and spaghetti, it is important to dry the sheets a little prior to cutting them. This takes 5–45 minutes depending on humidity, temperature and other weather conditions. If the sheets are cut while too wet, the pasta strips will stick together when drying or cooking. However, don't allow the pasta to dry out too much or it will break when cut.

The most basic pasta machines include cutting attachments for tagliolini and fettucine, and other attachments are sold for other types of pasta. Widths vary significantly from region to region. Here is an approximate guide:

- Capellini – 1–2 mm wide
- Spaghetti and tagliolini – 2 mm wide
- Linguini – 4 mm wide
- Tagliatelle – 6 mm wide
- Fettucine – 8 mm wide
- Pappardelle – 30 mm wide

—MAKES approximately 600 g (1 lb 5 oz)

SQUID (OR CUTTLEFISH) INK
FRESH EGG PASTA DOUGH

Prep Time 1 hour, plus 30 minutes chilling

Combine the flour, semolina and sea salt and place on a work surface or large wooden board. The flour should form a peaked mound. With your hand, make a hole in the top of the mound so that it resembles a volcano. This hole needs to be big enough to house the eggs.

Break the eggs into the hole. Combine the squid ink with 1 teaspoon water and add to the eggs. With your hands or with a fork, gently beat the ink and egg mixture, then slowly incorporate the flour. This can be done by moving your hand in a circular motion, slowly incorporating the flour from the inside wall of the mound. Don't worry if the dough looks like a mess: this is normal. Once fully combined, knead a bit more flour into the dough if it feels a little wet and sticky. Set the dough aside and clean the work space.

Dust flour onto the work surface and continue kneading the dough for 5 minutes. Wrap the dough in plastic and refrigerate for at least 30 minutes.

Roll the pasta to the desired thickness and cut into the desired shape (see Fresh egg pasta dough opposite).

Note
Both squid and cuttlefish ink make good black pasta and can be substituted for each other. Ink products sold in jars are the most convenient source. However, you can obtain it from both fresh cuttlefish and squid as it is contained in the silver/black sacs inside the seafood. Extracting it will take a little practice, but it is a great source of ink.

—MAKES approximately 600 g (1 lb 5 oz)

330 g (2¼ cups) plain flour, plus extra for kneading and rolling
70 g (⅓ cup) fine semolina
½ teaspoon fine sea salt
3 × 60 g (2 oz) free-range eggs
2 tablespoons squid/cuttlefish ink

MAYONNAISE

Prep Time 15 minutes

Place the egg yolks, mustard, salt and vinegar in a mixing bowl and then slowly whisk in the oil to emulsify. Store in an airtight container in the fridge for up to 1 week.

—MAKES 1.1 litres (4¼ cups)

6 egg yolks
1 tablespoon Dijon mustard
1 pinch salt
100 ml (scant ½ cup) white wine vinegar
1 litre (4 cups) vegetable oil

BASE RECIPES

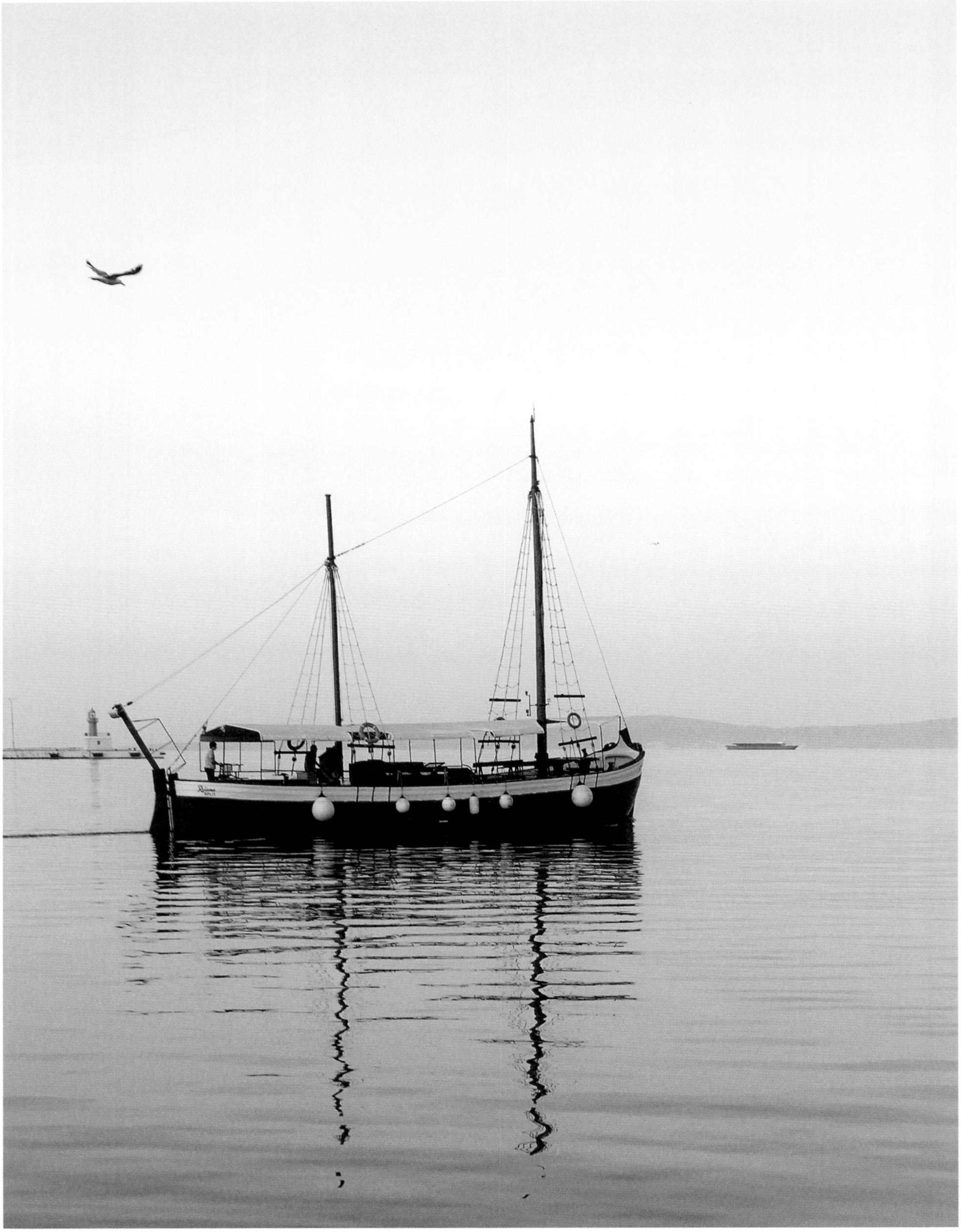

HOUSE-MADE BUTTER/BUTTERMILK

Prep Time 30 minutes

900 ml (3¾ cups) thick
 (double) cream
1 tablespoon sea salt

To make butter, place the cream in a mixing bowl and whisk until the buttermilk separates from the butter solids.

Drain the buttermilk and reserve. You will be left with approximately 400 g (14 oz) butter. Place the butter into a muslin cloth and rinse under cold running water until all the remaining buttermilk has been removed.

Wring the butter in a clean muslin cloth to remove as much of the remaining liquid as possible.

While the butter is still soft, mix in the salt in a dry mixing bowl and store in an airtight container in the fridge for 2–3 weeks.

—MAKES approximately 360 g (13 oz) butter

—MAKES approximately 475 ml (scant 2 cups) buttermilk

MASCARPONE

Prep Time 5 minutes, plus cooling and overnight resting
Cooking Time 30–60 minutes

250 ml (1 cup) thick
 (double) cream
1 tablespoon lemon juice

Place the cream in a saucepan and, using a cooking thermometer, bring it to 88°C (190°F) over a medium-high heat. When the cream is at temperature, lower the heat and maintain the 88°C (190°F) temperature.

Add the lemon juice to the cream and stir through until it thickens enough to coat the back of a wooden spoon.

Remove from the heat and allow to cool for 30 minutes.

Place three layers of muslin cloth inside a fine strainer and place over a bowl. When the mix is cold, pour into the strainer, then cover well and leave overnight.

Take the mascarpone out of the strainer and store in an airtight container in the refrigerator for up to 5 days.

—MAKES approximately 100 g (scant ½ cup)

ACKNOWLEDGEMENTS

Cookbooks are a massive undertaking and require the help and collaboration of a lot of people. I am deeply indebted to many and will attempt to name them all here. No doubt I will miss important people: I apologise in advance.

Firstly, thanks must start with Danielle Bowling, a shadow writer extraordinaire and very talented person who managed to put up with my scattered energy and historical 'poetic license' like few would. Without her, this magnificent book simply wouldn't exist.

To Dean Worthy – The Restaurant Pendolino's head chef – another talented professional whose collaboration made creating this book a great pleasure. He was dragged halfway across the globe to complete the research and I am very grateful for the excellence of his work, often under trying circumstances. It is appreciated.

Mark Beattie, a dear friend and colleague, an industry professional and fellow chef of the highest calibre, who really enabled me to do the crazy travelling and research that this book required. With tireless energy and an educated and keen critical eye, he is a person who only adds to the quality of any undertaking he is involved in. A first-rate human to boot. We are eternally grateful.

The teams at the restaurants: in particular Aimee, Maggi, Nic, Santosh, Loic and many more. Lilet and Peter for helping with the recipe testing. Special thanks, again, to Raffaello Pignetti for the ongoing intellectual input that continues to colour our days. To the non-executive restaurant team, Leon Young, John Malolakis and Sam Kitchen, it goes without saying but the support is immensely appreciated.

To the two amazingly talented photographers: Andrea Butti in Italy, location photographer, you're not family but you might as well be; and Alan Benson for such amazing studio shots. Gifted craftsmen.

Food stylist – Vanessa Austin, who's an absolute joy to work with. We're simply very grateful for the quality of the composition and for how quickly and enthusiastically you embraced this book's concept.

The team at Murdoch: Corinne Roberts, Vivien Valk, Jane Price, Kay Halsey and Lou Johnson, a very big thank you for a great collaboration.

To the people on the ground in Venice and in the greater Venetian Republic. Firstly the wine producers – Degani, Cavazza and La Farra – we are grateful for your long-standing support and the quality of what you do. To the Quintarelli family, thank you for so generously welcoming us into your extraordinary world. Time at Quintarelli is a sacred experience and is life changing for anyone truly interested in quality and craftsmanship. Grazie mille.

To some of the best restaurateurs in the business: the famous Mauro Lorenzon from L'Enoiteca Mascareta and Luca Di Vita from Osteria alle Testiere.

And to the Republic's Michelin culinary elite: Giancarlo Perbellini and the Alajmo brothers. These guys give cutting-edge context to an ever-evolving food culture in one of the most important culinary regions in the world. Extraordinary hospitality and enlightening dining experiences.

To Petros Markantonatos and the Gentilini family, from the Gentilini winery in Cephalonia. Spearheading the exciting 'new' frontier in wine and food from the most ancient of lands, your help and guidance is deeply appreciated.

Nic, Pia and Matilda in Milan. Thank you for the heartfelt friendship and shared passion for all things Italian, food, wine and music, and for the last-minute bed after a 24-hour haul from Sydney – appreciated.

On the ground in Australia, special thanks to David Tsirekas, my 'brother' from the 'other' culture and John Pye for the input on the recipes – much appreciated. Mitch and Mark, gratitude forever. To the crazy Veneta from Adelaide, Sandra Dei Poi – the support has been immense.

Thanks also to Luke Nguyen for the initial encouragement to become a cookbook author.

To my immediate and extended families – brothers, cousins, uncles and aunties – the Zoccali and Prowse clans and to the Syrmis and Moraitis clans. The support is always felt and is always appreciated. A very special mention to my mother-in law, Maria Syrmis, and her family – my in-laws on Ithaca. I'm very grateful for the support, the memories and the important input to this book.

And still on the subject of family, whilst not Venetian, my father, Domenico Zoccali, is an influence that lingers long and deep like a Giuseppe Quintarelli Amarone – grazie, papa.

Now for the three people who have really inspired this cookbook: Cristian, Ino and Krissoula.

To Ino and Marianna Kuvacic, dear friends who have given much wisdom over many years, and context to the stunning place that is the Croatian coast. Thanks for your passion and enthusiasm and for seeding the concept of this book. You are inspiring people, deeply connečtéd to your amazing history. It's a pleasure to know you and we are deeply grateful.

Cristian Casarin. Where do I start? Loud, passionate, loyal, knowledgeable, extremely funny, extremely Venetian – and strangely, a bloody Aussie too. The restaurant group sommelier, born in Noale, 30 kilometres from Venice but having made Sydney his home for some 20 years. We thank you for everything you've done; it's just been such a pleasure to do great work with you, and to do it together. Thanks also to your mum and dad, Mario and Rosalia, and for my favourite risotto of all time.

Krissoula, well, after 20 years of marriage here it is – Greece finally meets Italy in the most relevant of ways. Some have called you Penelope; I call you my beautiful, wise partner. And what a partnership. I love every bit of you, everything you believe in and stand for.

And now for the last two.

Thanks to my son, Luca, just for being who you are and for believing in your dad.

Lastly to my mother, Norma, for all the hard work and belief over many years: it will always be appreciated. The book is dedicated to you.

ACKNOWLEDGEMENTS

INDEX

Published in 2019 by Murdoch Books, an imprint of Allen & Unwin

Murdoch Books Australia
83 Alexander Street, Crows Nest NSW 2065
Phone: +61 (0)2 8425 0100
murdochbooks.com.au
info@murdochbooks.com.au

Murdoch Books UK
Ormond House, 26–27 Boswell Street,
London, WC1N 3JZ
Phone: +44 (0) 20 8785 5995
murdochbooks.co.uk
info@murdochbooks.co.uk

For corporate orders & custom publishing contact our business development team
at salesenquiries@murdochbooks.com.au

Publisher: Corinne Roberts
Editorial Manager: Jane Price
Creative Manager: Vivien Valk
Editor: Kay Halsey
Designer: Lucy Sykes-Thompson
Location photography: Andrea Butti
Food photography: Alan Benson
Styling: Vanessa Austin
Food preparation for photography: Dean Worthy
Production Director: Lou Playfair

ISBN 978 1 76052 387 9 Australia
ISBN 978 1 91163 208 5 UK

A catalogue record for this
book is available from the
National Library of Australia

A catalogue record for this book is available from the British Library

Colour reproduction by Splitting Image Colour Studio Pty Ltd, Clayton, Victoria
Printed by C & C Offset Printing Co Ltd, China

TABLESPOON MEASURES: We have used Australian 20 ml (4 teaspoon) tablespoon
measures. If you are using a smaller European 15 ml (3 teaspoon) tablespoon, add an
extra teaspoon of the ingredient for each tablespoon specified.

MIX
Paper from
responsible sources
FSC® C008047

The paper in this book is FSC® certified.
FSC® promotes environmentally responsible,
socially beneficial and economically viable
management of the world's forests.